Twentieth Edition

THE 2000 CALIFORNIA NOTARY LAW PRIMER

All the hard-to-find information every California Notary Public needs to know!

National Notary Association

Published by:

National Notary Association
9350 De Soto Avenue, P.O. Box 2402
Chatsworth, CA 91313-2402
1-818-739-4000
Fax: 1-818-700-0920
www.nationalnotary.org
E-mail: nna@nationalnotary.org

Twentieth Edition
First Edition © 1978

ISBN No. 1-891133-20-9
ISSN No. 1096-9985

Table of Contents

Introduction

You are to be commended on your interest in California Notary law! Purchasing *The California Notary Law Primer* identifies you as a conscientious professional who takes your official responsibilities seriously.

In few fields is the expression "more to it than meets the eye" truer than in Notary law. What often appears on the surface to be a simple procedure may, in fact, have important legal considerations.

The purpose of *The California Notary Law Primer* is to provide you with a resource to help decipher the many intricate laws that affect notarization. In so doing, the *Primer* will acquaint you with all important aspects of California's Notary law and with prudent notarial practices in general.

This 2000 edition of *The California Notary Law Primer* has been updated to include all recent pertinent law changes, including legislation enacted in 1998 that:

- Specifically outlaws use of the term *Notario Publico*;

- Requires the Secretary of State to revoke the commission of a Notary for certain advertising violations on the second occurrence; and

- Sets limits on the Notary's ability to assist others with immigration forms.

While *The California Notary Law Primer* begins with informative chapters on how to obtain your commission, what tools the Notary needs, often-asked questions, and critical steps in notarization, the heart of this book is the chapter entitled "Notary Laws Explained." Here, we take you through the myriad of Notary laws and put them in easy-to-understand terms. Every section of the law is analyzed and explained, as well as topics not covered by California law but nonetheless of vital concern to you as a Notary.

For handy reference, we have reprinted the pertinent text of the laws of California that relate to Notaries Public. In addition, we have included addresses and phone numbers of Secretary of State offices, County Clerk offices and Bureaus of Vital Statistics, plus a list of nations that are parties to the Hague Convention, a treaty which simplifies the process of authentication.

Whether you're about to be commissioned for the first time, or a longtime Notary, we're sure *The California Notary Law Primer* will provide you with new insights and understanding. Your improved comprehension of California's Notary law will naturally result in greater competence as a professional Notary Public.

Milton G. Valera
President
National Notary Association

How to Become a California Notary Public

1. Ensure that you comply with the basic qualifications for a California Notary commission.

First, you must be a legal resident of the state. Second, you must be 18 years of age or older. And third, you must not have been convicted of a felony or of a crime involving moral turpitude.

U.S. citizenship is not required as long as you legally reside in this country under federal law. There is no minimum time of state residency — you can apply for a commission on the same day you enter California. A "legal resident" is a person who is residing in the state and who intends to stay, as indicated usually by taking action to obtain a driver's license, registering to vote or the like.*

2. Obtain a commission application and Notary exam registration instructions.

Whether you are applying for a Notary commission for the first time or you are renewing your commission, you must pass a written and proctored examination administered at designated sites throughout California.

To receive a commission application and instructions on registering for the exam, call Cooperative Personnel Services (CPS)** at 1-916-263-3520, Monday through Saturday, 6 a.m. to 7 p.m. Exams are also offered following National Notary Association seminars. Call the NNA at 1-800-876-6827 for

---

*California may also appoint Notaries to act only on a given U.S. military base. The applicant must be a U.S. citizen, a federal civil servant and recommended by the commanding officer of the base. Such four-year commissions terminate when employment on the base ends.

**Cooperative Personnel Services is a private firm, contracted by the Secretary of State to administer California's Notary Public exam at sites throughout the state.

information or to sign up for a seminar and exam. Usually within a week of calling CPS or the NNA, you will receive an official Notary commission application, exam registration instructions, a list of exam dates and a *California Notary Public Handbook*.

To avoid a gap between commissions, renewing Notaries should begin the application process five months before their commissions expire. Renewal applications will not be accepted earlier than six months before expiration.

3. Study the Notary Public Handbook.

The 25-question, multiple-choice exam is based on the *California Notary Public Handbook,* which should be studied thoroughly. It is also helpful to review the "Notary Laws Explained" chapter of this *Primer*, starting on page 18.

4. Have your fingerprints taken.

All first-time applicants must be fingerprinted. Notaries with current commissions and ex-Notaries whose commissions have not lapsed for more than three months do not need to be fingerprinted again.

The required fingerprints may be taken at a variety of places, but you must ensure that a "BID-7 card" is used. Prints may be taken at a state Department of Real Estate office, at most sheriff's and police stations, or at private fingerprinting and passport service businesses. Of course, a fee will be charged. If you have trouble getting a fingerprint card, contact the Secretary of State's Notary Public Section at 1-916-653-3595. The National Notary Association also provides fingerprint cards and kits. To order, call 1-800-876-6827.

Both sides of the print card must be filled out, including your signature and that of the print-taker. "Application for Notary Public Commission" must be clearly written on the card. Avoid smearing the prints. Do not fold the card.

5. Complete the application.

Follow the clear instructions on the reverse side of the application. Be aware that any false statements or omission of any information required by this form is cause for denial of a Notary commission.

6. Register for the exam.

Select a convenient site and time, and register for the exam, following the instructions provided. You may register by mail at least 11 business days prior to the requested exam date, or by calling 1-916-263-3520. You may also show up at an exam site without registering beforehand, but there would be no guarantee of a space for you.

A confirmation letter for the exam will be sent to you if your registration is received at least 11 business days prior to the exam date. Most exam takers will have little difficulty finding their exam site, since the exams are administered at well-known colleges, high schools and community centers.

Exams following NNA seminars are also easy to find, as the seminars are held at well-known hotels. To sign up for an NNA seminar and the following state exam, call 1-800-876-6827.

7. Take the exam.

Report to the selected site 60 minutes before the designated exam time. For walk-ins, the policy is first-come, first-served.

Be prepared to present:

- Identification — a valid California driver's license, a nondriver's ID or a current U.S. or foreign passport.

- Commission fees — a check or money order (payable to "Secretary of State") with your printed name and Social Security number written on the lower left side. Each applicant must have a separate check or money order. For first-time applicants, the fee is $72. For applicants who currently hold California Notary commissions or whose commissions have expired within the previous three months, the fee is $40. However, Notaries whose commissions have been expired longer than three months must pay $72, which includes $40 for commissioning and $32 for a new fingerprint analysis.

- A completed application form.

- A completed fingerprint card, if required.

- Two sharp #2 black lead pencils.

You will be given 45 minutes to take the exam. Wallets, credit cards, keys and IDs are allowed at the testing tables, provided they are kept in a clear, sealed plastic bag. All other items, such as backpacks, purses and books must be kept at the back of the room once testing begins. Because neither CPS nor the NNA can be responsible for lost or stolen property, it is recommended that you leave these belongings in your locked car.

Within 10 business days after the exam, you'll be informed by mail whether you passed or failed. Scores will not be released or discussed over the telephone. If you pass the exam, your application materials will be forwarded to the Secretary of State. If you fail, you will receive instructions. You may take the exam again at a cost of $20, but not within the same calendar month.

Usually within four to six weeks, your application will be processed by the state, and your new Notary commission will be mailed to you, along with a list of licensed seal manufacturers and a Certificate of Authorization allowing you to purchase a seal. If you are a renewing Notary, the new commission will usually be sent to you approximately 30 days before your present commission expires, depending on when the application process was initiated.

8. File your bond and oath of office.

Within 30 calendar days of the starting date indicated on your commission, you must purchase a $15,000 Notary bond from a licensed surety firm. Both the bond and oath of office must be filed with the clerk of the county in which your principal place of business is located. This can be done either in person, or by certified mail if the oath is taken and subscribed before a Notary Public in the same county. Filing fees will vary by county. If you do not file within 30 days, your commission becomes invalid. In this case, you must complete a new application and mail it to the Secretary of State's Notary Public Section with a $20 fee; however, you do not have to take the exam again.

9. Purchase your official Notary seal.

To purchase an official seal, present or mail the Certificate of Authorization to a licensed seal manufacturer, who will make the seal, affix its impression on the certificate and then return the certificate to the state. You may start using this seal on or after your commission starting date, as long as you have filed your oath and bond with the County Clerk and have obtained a journal in which to record your notarial acts. ■

Tools
of the Trade

There are several tools that Notaries need to carry out their duties lawfully and efficiently. These tools are as important to the Notary as a hammer and saw are to the carpenter.

Inking Seal

The inking seal is the Notary's official seal. Its impression reproduces photographically, a legal requirement. All official acts are authenticated with this seal. It must include the Notary's name, the state seal, the words "Notary Public," the name of the county where the Notary's bond is filed, the expiration date of the Notary's commission, and identification numbers for both the Notary and the seal manufacturer or vendor.

Seal Embosser

While not required by California law, the seal embosser is used in many states and is often expected on documents sent abroad. Many California Notaries opt to affix an embossment in addition to the legally required inked-seal impression. The seal embosser makes a nonphotographically reproducible indentation on the document. Because photocopies of documents can sometimes easily pass as originals today, the embossment can be used to distinguish an original from a photocopy. Also, embossing all pages in a document together can safeguard against later substitution or addition of pages.

Journal of Notarial Acts

The Notary's journal is required by law. Each entry must include the date, time, and type of each official act; the type of document notarized; the signature of each person whose signature is notarized; the type of information used to verify the identity of the parties whose signatures are acknowledged; the fee charged; and, for deeds, quitclaim deeds and deeds of trust affecting real property, the right thumbprint of the signer. The Notary's journal provides a record of notarial transactions that may be used as evidence in a court proceeding.

Jurat Stamp

The jurat stamp impresses on an affidavit the jurat wording "Subscribed and sworn to before me this _____ day of _____, _____ by _____." The jurat stamp is more convenient (and safer, since critical wording will not be omitted) than typing the wording on each affidavit that requires it.

Venue Stamp

The venue stamp is used in conjunction with the jurat stamp in a jurat. The phrase, "State of _____, County of _____," indicates where the jurat was executed. Also usable for acknowledgments.

Fingerprinting Device

Since the signers of deeds, quitclaim deeds and deeds of trust affecting real property must leave a right thumbprint in a California Notary's journal, many Notaries opt for the convenience of an inexpensive fingerprinting device.

Notarial Certificates

Preprinted notarial certificates for acknowledgments, jurats, proofs of execution by subscribing witness, and for copy certification by document custodian are available.

Errors and Omissions Insurance

Notary errors and omissions insurance provides protection for Notaries who are sued for damages resulting from unintentional notarial mistakes. In the event of a lawsuit, the "E&O" insurance company will provide and pay for the Notary's legal counsel and absorb any damages levied by a court or agreed to in a settlement, up to the policy coverage limit. Errors and omissions insurance does not cover the Notary for intentional misconduct. ■

As a full-service organization, the National Notary Association makes available to California Notaries all notarial items required by law, custom and convenience.

10 Most-Asked Questions

Every Notary has a question or two about whether and how to notarize. But there are certain questions that pop up again and again. These top 10 are asked repeatedly at the National Notary Association's seminars, its annual National Conference of Notaries Public and through its *Notary Information Service.*

As with most questions about notarization, the answer is not always a simple "yes" or "no." Rather, the answer sometimes is, "It depends...."

Here's what every Notary wants to know:

1. Can I notarize a will?

In general, no. The *California Notary Public Handbook,* issued by the Secretary of State, recommends that any person requesting notarization of a will be asked to see an attorney.

Laws regarding wills differ from state to state. Some states do not require notarization of wills, while others allow it as one of several witnessing options. Usually, it is not the will itself that is notarized, but accompanying affidavits signed by witnesses.

A Notary should only notarize a document described as a will if clear instructions and a notarial certificate are provided. If the signer of the will is relying on the Notary for advice on how to proceed, the Notary should tell the individual to see an attorney.

The danger in notarizing wills is that would-be testators who have drafted their own wills without legal advice may believe that notarization will make their wills legal and valid. However, even when notarized, such homemade wills may be worthless because the testators failed to obtain the proper number of witnesses or omitted important information.

In fact, notarization itself may actually void an otherwise

properly executed handwritten (holographic) will, because courts have occasionally held that any writing on the document other than the testator's invalidates the will.

2. Can I notarize for a stranger with no identification?

Yes. If identification of a signer cannot be based on personal knowledge or identification documents (ID cards), a Notary may rely on the oath or affirmation of one personally known credible identifying witness, or two credible identifying witnesses who are strangers to the Notary but have acceptable identification themselves, to identify an unknown signer.

If one credible identifying witness is used, the California Notary must personally know the credible identifying witness, who must personally know the document signer. This establishes a chain of personal knowledge from the Notary to the credible identifying witness to the signer.

If two credible identifying witnesses are used, both must have proper identification, such as a valid state driver's license, a state nondriver's ID or a current passport. However, two credible identifying witnesses who are *not* personally known by the Notary may not be used to identify a subscribing witness in a proof of execution.

When no credible identifying witness is available to identify a stranger without IDs, the Notary may have no choice but to tell the signer to find a personally known Notary or a friend who personally knows a Notary, if the signer is unable to obtain an adequate identification document.

3. Can I notarize a photograph?

No. To simply stamp and sign a photograph is improper. A Notary's signature and seal must appear only on a notarial certificate (such as an acknowledgment or jurat) accompanying a written statement signed by another person.

However, a signature on a written statement referring to an accompanying or attached photograph may be notarized; if the photograph is large enough, the statement and notarial certificate might even appear on its reverse side. Such formats may be acceptable when notarized photos are requested by persons seeking medical or health licenses, or by legal resident aliens renewing foreign passports.

A word of caution here: a Notary should always be suspicious about notarizing a photo-bearing card or document that could be used as a bogus "official" ID.

4. What if there's no room for my seal or if it smears?

Usually, if notarial wording printed on a document leaves no room for a seal, a loose certificate can be attached and filled out instead, if the certificate wording is substantially the same as on the document.

If an initial seal impression is unreadable and there is ample room on the document, another impression can be affixed nearby. The illegibility of the first impression will indicate why a second seal impression was necessary. And the Notary should record in the journal that a second seal was applied.

A Notary should *never* attempt to fix an imperfect seal impression with pen, ink or correction fluid. This may be viewed as evidence of tampering and cause the document's rejection by a recorder.

5. Can I notarize signatures on faxes or photocopies of documents?

Yes. A photocopy may be notarized as long as it bears an *original* signature, meaning the photocopy must have been signed with pen and ink. A photocopied signature may *never* be notarized.

Similarly, a faxed document must be signed in ink. In addition, if a faxed document is on thermal paper (the slick paper typically used in fax machines), the document should be photocopied onto regular copy paper to avoid the fading of any printed matter and to allow the affixation of signatures and the Notary's seal.

Note that some public recorders may not accept notarized signatures on photocopied documents because they will not adequately reproduce in microfilming.

When carbon copies are made, the Notary will sometimes be asked to conform rather than to notarize the copies. To conform a copy, the Notary reaffixes the official seal on the copy (carbon will not readily transfer a seal impression) and writes "Conformed Copy" prominently across the copy.

6. May I notarize for customers only?

No. As a public official, a Notary is not commissioned to serve just the customers or clients of any one business, even when the employer has paid for the bond, commissioning fees and notarial supplies. There is no such officer as a "Notary Private."

It is ethically improper — although hardly ever explicitly prohibited by statute — to discriminate between customers and noncustomers in offering or refusing to offer notarial services and in charging or not charging fees.

Discrimination against anyone who presents a lawful request for notarization is not a suitable policy for a public official commissioned to serve all of the public equally. Also, such discrimination can provide the basis for lawsuits.

That said, California law does, however, have a provision whereby a Notary and employer may agree to limit the Notary's services to transactions directly related to the employer's business. This does not permit discrimination between customers and noncustomers, but only between business-related and nonbusiness-related documents.

7. Can I notarize a document in a language I can't read?

Yes. As long as the notarial certificate and document signature are in a language the Notary *can* read, California Notaries may notarize documents written in languages they *cannot* read.

However, there are certain difficulties and dangers in notarizing documents that the Notary cannot read. The main difficulty for the Notary is making an accurate journal description of an unreadable document; the main danger to the public and the Notary is that the document may be blatantly fraudulent.

Under no circumstances should a notarization be performed if the Notary and the principal signer cannot directly communicate in the same language.

8. Can I certify a copy of a birth certificate?

No. California Notaries are authorized to certify copies only of powers of attorney and, if requested by the Secretary of State, entries in their official journals of notarial acts.

Some states do allow Notaries to certify copies, but copies of documents that are either public records or publicly recordable should never be certified by Notaries. Only an officer in a bureau of vital statistics should certify a copy of a birth certificate or other vital public record; a Notary's "certification" of a birth or death record may actually lend credibility to a counterfeit or tampered document. Only a county recording official should certify a copy of a deed or other recordable instrument.

In states allowing Notary-certified copies, the types of documents that Notaries may properly certify copies of are original personal papers, such as letters and college diplomas, and in-house business documents.

9. Does a document have to be signed in my presence?

No and yes. Documents requiring acknowledgments normally do not need to be signed in the Notary's presence. However, the signer *must* appear before the Notary at the time of notarization to acknowledge that he or she freely signed for the purposes stated in the document.

An acknowledgment certificate indicates that the signer personally appeared before the Notary, was identified by the Notary, and acknowledged to the Notary that the document was freely signed.

On the other hand, documents requiring a jurat *must* indeed be signed in the Notary's presence, as dictated by the typical jurat wording, "Subscribed (signed) and sworn to before me...."

In executing a jurat, a Notary guarantees that the signer: personally appeared before the Notary, was given an oath or affirmation by the Notary, and signed in the Notary's presence. In addition, even though it may not be a statutory requirement that the Notary positively identify a signer for a jurat, it is always a good idea to do so.

10. Can I notarize for a family member?

Yes and no. Although California state law does not expressly prohibit notarizing for family members, Notaries who do so may violate the statutes prohibiting a direct beneficial interest — especially in notarizing for spouses in states, like California, with community property laws.

Besides the possibility of a financial interest in notarizing for a relative, there may be an "emotional interest" that can prevent the Notary from acting impartially. For example, a Notary who is asked to notarize a contract signed by his brother might attempt to persuade the sibling to sign or not sign. As a brother, the individual is entitled to exert influence — but this is entirely improper for a Notary.

Even if a Notary has no direct beneficial interest in the document and does not attempt to influence the signer, notarizing for a relative could subject the document to a legal challenge if other parties to the transaction allege that the Notary could not have acted impartially. ■

Steps to Proper Notarization

What constitutes reasonable care?

If a Notary can convincingly show that he or she used every reasonable precaution expected of a person of ordinary prudence and intelligence, then the Notary has exercised reasonable care — a shield against liability.

The following 14-step checklist will help Notaries apply reasonable care and avert the most common pitfalls.

1. Require every signer to personally appear.

The signer *must* appear in person before the Notary on the date and in the county stated in the notarial certificate. "Personal appearance" means the signer is in the Notary's physical presence — face to face in the same room. A telephone call is not acceptable as personal appearance.

2. Make a careful identification.

The Notary should identify every document signer through either personal knowledge, a credible identifying witness under oath, or reliable identification documents (ID cards).

When using ID cards, the Notary must examine them closely to detect alteration, counterfeiting or evidence that they are issued to an impostor. Don't rely on a type of card with which you are unfamiliar, unless you check it against a reference such as the *U.S. Identification Manual* or the *ID Checking Guide*.

3. Feel certain the signer understands the document.

A conscientious and careful Notary will be certain not only of the signer's identity and willingness to sign, but also will make a layperson's judgment about the signer's ability to understand the document. While California Notaries are not expressly required by law to determine "competence," it is in the Notary's best interest to make a commonsense judgment about the signer's awareness.

A document signer who cannot respond intelligibly in a simple conversation with the Notary should not be considered lucid enough to sign at that moment. If in doubt, the Notary can ask the signer if he or she understands the document and can explain its purpose. Or, if in a medical environment, the signer's doctor can be consulted for a professional opinion.

4. Check the signature.

The Notary must make sure that the document signer signs the same name appearing on the identification presented.

To check for possible forgery, the Notary should compare the signature that the person leaves in the journal of notarial acts against the signatures on the document and on the IDs. Also, it should be noted whether the signer appears to be laboring on the journal signature, a possible indication of forgery in progress.

Generally, an abbreviated form of a name (John D. Smith instead of John David Smith, for example), is acceptable. However, deviation is only allowed if the individual is signing with *less* than and not *more* than what is on the identification document.

5. Look for blank spaces.

California Notaries are expressly prohibited by law from notarizing incomplete documents.

Documents with blank spaces have a great potential for fraudulent misuse. A borrower, for example, might sign an incomplete promissory note, trusting the lender to fill it out, and then later find that the lender has written in an amount in excess of what was actually borrowed.

If the blanks are inapplicable and intended to be left unfilled, the signer should be asked to line through each space (using ink), or to write in "Not Applicable" or "NA."

6. Scan the document.

Notaries are not required to read the documents they notarize. However, they should note certain important particulars about a document, such as its title, for recording in the journal of notarial acts. Notaries may also count and record the number of pages; this can show whether pages are later fraudulently added or removed.

7. Check the document's date.

For acknowledgments, the date of signing on the document must either precede or be the same as the date of the notarization but not follow it. For a jurat, the document signing date and the notarization date must be the same.

A document dated to follow the date on its notarial certificate risks rejection by a recorder, who may question how the document could have been notarized before it was signed.

8. Keep a journal of notarial acts.

A journal is mandatory for all Notaries in California. If a notarized document is lost or altered, or if certain facts about the transaction are later challenged, the Notary's journal becomes valuable evidence. It can protect the rights of all parties to a transaction and help Notaries defend themselves against false accusations.

The Notary should include *all* the pertinent details of the notarization in the journal: the date, time and type of notarization, the date and type of document, the signature, printed name and address of the signer (and any witnesses), how this person was identified and notarial fees charged, if any. In addition, signers of deeds affecting real property must leave a right thumbprint in the Notary's journal. Any other pertinent data, such as the capacity the signer is claiming, may also be entered.

9. Complete the journal entry first.

The Notary should complete the journal entry entirely *before* filling out the notarial certificate. This prevents a signer from leaving before the important public record of the notarization is made in the journal.

10. Make sure the document has notarial wording.

If a notarial certificate does not come with the document, the Notary must ask the document signer what type of notarization — acknowledgment, jurat or other — is required. The Notary may then type the appropriate notarial wording on the document or attach a preprinted, "loose" certificate.

If the signer does not know what type of notarization is required, he or she should contact the document's issuing or receiving agency to determine this. This decision is *never* the Notary's to make unless the Notary is also an attorney.

11. Be attentive to details.

When filling out the certificate, the Notary needs to make sure the venue correctly identifies the place of notarization; if the venue is preprinted and incorrect, the Notary must line through the incorrect state and/or county, write in the proper site of the notarization and initial the change.

Also, the Notary must pay attention to spaces on the notarial certificate that indicate the number and gender of the document signers, as well as how they were identified — for example, leave the plural "(s)" untouched or cross it out, as appropriate.

12. Affix your signature and seal properly.

Notaries should sign *exactly* the same name appearing on their commissioning papers. And they must never forget to affix their official seals — a common reason for rejection of a document by a recorder.

The seal should be placed as close to the Notary's signature as possible without overprinting it. To prevent illegibility, a Notary seal should not be affixed over wording, particularly over a signature.

13. Protect 'loose' certificates.

If the Notary has to attach a notarial certificate, it must be securely stapled to the left margin of the document. Notaries can protect against the removal of such attachments by embossing them together with the document and writing the particulars of the document to which the certificate is attached on the certificate. For example, the notation, "This certificate is attached to a 15-page partnership agreement between John Smith and Mary Doe, signed July 14, 1997," would deter fraudulent removal and reattachment of a loose certificate.

14. Don't give advice.

Every state prohibits nonattorneys from practicing law. Notaries should *never* prepare or complete documents for others, nor give advice on any matter relating to a document unless they are attorneys or professionals certified or licensed in a relevant area of expertise. The nonattorney Notary *never* chooses the type of certificate or notarization a document needs, since this decision can have important legal ramifications. The Notary could be held liable for any damages resulting from an incorrectly chosen certificate or notarization. ■

Notary Laws Explained

In layperson's language, this chapter discusses and clarifies key parts of the laws of California that regulate Notaries Public. Most of these laws are reprinted in full in "California Laws Pertaining to Notaries Public" beginning on page 79.

This edition explains the changes to California law that were enacted in 1998 and take effect January 1, 1999.

Notable among these changes were new provisions that: prohibit the use of the term *Notario Public*; require the Secretary of State to revoke a Notary's commission for certain advertising violations on the second occurrence; and set limits on the Notary's ability to assist others with immigration forms.

THE NOTARY COMMISSION

Application for Commission

Qualifications. To become a Notary in California, the applicant: (Government Code, Sections 8201, 8201.1, 8214.1)

1) Must be a legal California resident, or a federal civil servant on a military base in accord with Government Code, Section 8203.1;

2) Must be at least 18 years old;

3) Must complete and pass a proctored, written examination prescribed by the Secretary of State;

4) Must complete a fingerprint card to be used by the Secretary of State in reviewing the background of the applicant;

5) Must satisfy the Secretary of State that the applicant is a person of honesty and integrity, and must not have been convicted of a felony or of a crime involving moral turpitude;

6) Is expected to be able to read, write and understand the English language;

7) Is expected to have sufficient vision to read printed matter.

State-Residency Requirements. To become a Notary in California, the applicant must be a "legal resident" of the state. State officials maintain that a "legal resident" is a person who demonstrates the intent to permanently reside in the state by registering to vote or obtaining a California driver's license.

Citizenship. U.S. citizenship is not required to become a California Notary, though any noncitizen applicant should be a legally residing alien. A 1984 U.S. Supreme Court decision, *Bernal v. Fainter*, declared that no state may deny a Notary commission merely on the basis of lack of U.S. citizenship.

Application Fee. The fee for a first-time Notary commission applicant is $72. Of this, $32 is applied toward processing the applicant's fingerprints. Notaries who apply for a new commission before or within three months after their current commission expires need pay only $40, because they do not have to be fingerprinted again. Beyond three months, however, a new set of fingerprints is required and the application fee is again $72.

Application Misstatement. Substantial and material misstatement or omission in the application for a Notary commission is reason for the Secretary of State to refuse to grant or to revoke or suspend a Notary's commission. (Government Code, Section 8214.1)

Delinquency on Child Support Payments. The Secretary of State is prohibited from issuing or renewing a Notary commission for any person who has not complied with child support orders. Any commission fees that have been paid by the applicant will not be refunded. (Welfare and Institutions Code, Section 11350.6)

Dishonored Check. The Secretary of State may cancel the commission of a Notary Public if any of the commission fees are not paid due to a returned check. Upon receiving notice from a financial institution that a check or draft was not honored, the Secretary of State will notify the applicant and request payment by cashier's check. Should the Secretary of State need to issue a second notice, the commission will be cancelled effective the date of that second notice. (Government Code, Section 8204.1)

Examination

Required. All Notary commission applicants — including renewing Notaries — must complete and pass a proctored, written examination prescribed by the Secretary of State.

Cooperative Personnel Services (CPS), a private organization contracted by the state, administers the proctored exam at sites throughout California. For information about taking the exam, contact CPS at 1-916-263-3520. Or call the NNA at 1-800-876-6827 for information about taking the exam following an NNA seminar.

Fingerprints

Commission Applicants Are Fingerprinted. All first-time California Notary commission applicants must be fingerprinted. Of the $72 commission fee, $32 is applied toward processing of the applicant's fingerprints. Renewing California Notaries need not be fingerprinted again if the application is submitted before commission expiration or within three months afterward; in such cases, the renewal fee is $40. (Government Code, Section 8201.1)

How to Obtain Fingerprints. The National Notary Association provides required "BID-7" cards in an inkless Fingerprint Kit allowing applicants to take their own prints. These kits may be purchased by calling 1-800-876-6827.

For a fee, any state Department of Real Estate office, most police stations and passport service businesses will take fingerprints. There are also private fingerprinting services which can be located in the telephone book, usually listed under "Identification." If unable to obtain a valid fingerprint card, prospective and renewing Notaries may contact the Secretary of State's Notary Public Division for assistance at 1-916-653-3595.

Notary Bond

Requirement. California Notaries commissioned on or after January 1, 1997, are required to obtain a bond of $15,000 and file it at the office of the County Clerk in the county of their principal place of business. Notaries commissioned prior to January 1, 1997, are not required to increase their $10,000 bond until they renew their commissions. (Government Code, Section 8212)

Filing the Bond. The bond must be filed — and the oath of office taken (see "Oath of Office," page 22) — within 30 calendar days from the beginning of the Notary's term. Effective January 1, 1997, Notaries may file their bonds in person or by certified mail. The Notary commission does not take effect until the oath and bond are filed. The filing fee will vary by county.

The County Clerk forwards to the Secretary of State a copy of the Notary's oath and a certificate indicating that the bond was filed. The County Clerk then delivers the bond to the County Recorder for recording, after which the County Recorder mails the bond to the Notary. The Notary should keep the bond in a safe place for at least six years — the statutory limitation for lawsuits resulting from a notarial act — after the last notarial act performed. (Government Code, Section 8213)

Surety. The surety for the Notary's bond must be an approved, state-licensed bonding company. A deposit of funds may not be made in lieu of a surety bond. (Government Code, Section 8212)

Protects Public. The Notary bond protects the public from a Notary's misconduct or negligence; it does *not* protect the Notary. The bond provides coverage for damages to anyone who suffers financially due to an impropriety on the part of a Notary — intentional or not. The surety company will seek compensation from the Notary for any damages it has to pay out on the Notary's behalf. The Secretary of State is authorized to require the Notary to purchase replacement bonding if the original $15,000 bond funds are depleted by damage claims.

Liable for All Damages. Both the Notary and surety company may be sued for damages resulting from notarial misconduct. The surety is liable only up to the amount of the bond, but the Notary may be found liable for any amount of money. (Government Code, Section 8214)

Surety's Release from Obligation. If a surety feels that a Notary is likely to perform improper notarial acts in the future, the surety can appeal to the Superior Court for release from the obligation to bond the Notary. A judge may then require proof of the Notary's ability to obtain another surety. If the Notary neglects or refuses to provide a new surety, the Notary's commission may be revoked. (Government Code, Section 8216)

Oath of Office

Requirement. California Notaries are required to take an oath of office and file it with the County Clerk in the same county as their principal place of business. (Government Code, Sections 8212 and 8213)

Filing the Oath. The oath must be taken — and the Notary bond filed (see "Notary Bond," pages 20–22) — within 30 days from the beginning of the Notary's term. The Notary commission does not take effect until this is done. Notaries may take and file the oath in person at the County Clerk's office. Or the oath may be taken before another Notary Public in the same county where it will be filed and mailed by certified mail, along with the proper filing fee, to the County Clerk. Filing fees will vary by county. For a listing of County Clerks, see pages 105–107. (Government Code, Section 8213)

Jurisdiction

Statewide. Notaries may perform official acts throughout the state of California but not beyond the state borders. A Notary may not witness a signing outside California and then return to the state to perform the notarization; all parts of a notarial act must be performed at the same time and place within the state of California. (Government Code, Section 8200)

Term of Office

Four-Year Term. Beginning with the date specified on the commission certificate, a Notary's term of office is four years. The commission ends at midnight on the expiration date. (Government Code, Section 8204)

Reappointment

Application for Renewal. To avoid a gap between commissions, Notaries seeking reappointment should begin the application process five months before their commissions expire. Renewal applications will not be accepted earlier than six months before expiration. Applications are available from the

National Notary Association by calling 1-800-876-6827, or from Cooperative Personnel Services by calling 1-916-263-3520.

Fingerprints. Notaries applying for reappointment need not submit new fingerprints *if* the Notary's previous commission has not lapsed for more than three months. If expired more than three months, the applicant must submit new fingerprints as if applying for the first time. (Government Code, Section 8201.1) (See "Fingerprints," page 20.)

Commission Fees. For applicants who currently hold a California Notary commission or whose commission has expired within the previous three months, the fee is $40. However, for Notaries whose commissions have been expired for longer than three months, the fee is the same as if applying for the first time, $72, which includes the $40 commissioning fee and $32 for a new fingerprint analysis.

Exam Required. All new and renewing Notaries must complete and pass a written examination prescribed by the Secretary of State. (See "Examination," page 20.)

Journal. All California Notaries must maintain a journal of notarial acts for as long as they hold a Notary Public commission. (Government Code, Section 8206)
Renewing Notaries may continue recording their acts in the journal from their previous commission but should make a notation in the journal when the renewed commission begins.

Oath. The oath of office must be taken — and the Notary bond filed — within 30 days from the beginning of the Notary's new commission. The new commission does not take effect until this is done. (Government Code, Section 8213)

Bond. All Notaries commissioned on or after January 1, 1997 must obtain a $15,000 bond. (Government Code, Section 8212) (See "Notary Bond," pages 20–22.)

Seal. Renewing Notaries must destroy or deface the seal from their previous commission and obtain a new seal for the new commission. The procedures are the same as if obtaining a seal for the first time. (See "Notary Seal," pages 51–53.)

Resignation

Procedure. To resign, a Notary should immediately notify the Secretary of State by certified mail, destroy or deface the Notary seal and deliver the journal within 30 days to the County Clerk of the county where the Notary's bond and oath of office are filed. (See "Disposal of Notary Records," page 48.) (Government Code, Section 8209)

Death of Notary

Disposition of Notary Records. In the case of a Notary's death, the personal representative of the Notary must notify the Secretary of State and deliver all notarial records to the County Clerk of the county where the Notary's bond and oath of office are filed. (Government Code, Section 8209)

Public-Employee Notaries

Terms of Appointment. The Secretary of State may appoint and issue a Notary commission to state, county, city and public school district employees to act for the agencies in which they are employed. The employing agency may pay the premium on the Notary's bond and the cost of other required supplies from public funds at its disposal. (Government Code, Section 8202.5)

No Commission Fees. When a public employee applies for a Notary commission, a signed statement is required from an authorized representative of the agency in which the Notary's services are needed. Provided this statement is filed, no state or county appointment or filing fees need be paid. (Government Code, Section 8202.5)

Notary Fees. Any fees collected by a public-employee Notary must be turned over to the agency for which the Notary works. The agency is required to deposit these fees into the same fund from which the Notary's salary is paid. (Government Code, Section 8202.5)

Change of Address

Notification. The Secretary of State must be notified within 30 days by certified mail of a change in a Notary's principal place of business or residence address. (Government Code, Section 8213.5)

Refiled Oath and Bond. Since a Notary has statewide

jurisdiction and may notarize in any county, the Notary is not required to refile the oath of office and bond, even if his or her principal place of business moves to a new county. However, the Notary may elect to refile the oath of office and bond in the county of the new principal place of business. The Notary must then also obtain a new official seal within 30 days that reflects the change. (Government Code, Section 8213)

Change of Name

Notification Optional. A Notary who changes his or her name during the term of the Notary commission may continue to perform notarial acts under the previous name until his or her current commission expires. When the Notary renews his or her commission, the new name must be used and the previous name indicated on the commission application.

If a Notary wants to perform notarial acts with a new name before commission renewal, a change of name form must be filed with the Secretary of State. The Secretary of State will issue an amended commission with the Notary's new name. The amended commission takes effect on the date the oath and amendment to the bond (see following) are filed with the County Clerk. The Notary's commission term and commission number remain the same. (Government Code, Sections 8213 and 8213.6)

File New Oath and Bond Amendment. After a change of name application is filed, the Notary must also file, within 30 days of the date the amended commission is issued, a new oath of office and an amendment to the bond. The new oath and amended bond are filed with the County Clerk of the county in which the Notary's principal place of business is located. The amended commission will not take effect unless the filing is done within the 30-day period. (Government Code, Section 8213)

If the address of the Notary's principal place of business was also changed in the application for name change form, either a new or duplicate of the original bond must be filed with the County Clerk with the amendment to the bond. (Government Code, Section 8213)

New Seal. Within 30 days of filing the new oath and amended bond, the Notary must obtain a new official seal that reflects the name change — and county change, if applicable. (Government Code, Section 8213)

OFFICIAL NOTARIAL ACTS

Authorized Acts

Notaries may perform the following notarizations: (Government Code, Section 8205)

- Acknowledgments, certifying that a signer personally appeared before the Notary, was identified by the Notary, and acknowledged signing the document. (See pages 27–30.)

- Copy of Notarial Record. When asked by the state, Notaries must, within 30 days, send a certified copy of any requested journal entry. (See pages 30–31.)

- Certified Copy of Power of Attorney. Notaries may certify that a copy of a power of attorney document is identical to the original. (See pages 31–32.) (Probate Code, Section 4307)

- Depositions, certifying that the spoken words of a witness in a legal matter were accurately taken down in writing, though this act is most often done by skilled court reporters. (See pages 33–34.)

- Jurats, as found in affidavits and other sworn documents, certifying that the signer personally appeared before the Notary, signed in the Notary's presence, and took an oath or affirmation from the Notary. (See pages 34–36.)

- Oaths and Affirmations, which are solemn promises to God (oath) or solemn promises on one's own personal honor (affirmation). (See pages 36–38.)

- Proofs of Execution, certifying that a subscribing witness personally appeared and swore to the Notary that another person, the principal, signed a document. (See pages 38–40.)

- Protests, certifying that a written promise to pay, such as a bill of exchange, was not honored. (See pages 40–41.)

Unauthorized Acts

Notary's Own Signature. Notaries are not permitted to notarize their own signatures. (Government Code, Section 8224.1)

Certified Copies. A certified copy is a duplicate of an original document that is certified as an exact reproduction. In California, a Notary is prohibited from making certified copies of anything but the Notary's own official journal or a power of attorney document. (Government Code, Section 8205) (See "Certified Copies of Powers of Attorney," pages 31–32.)

Requests for certified copies of any other document should be directed to the agency that holds the original document. For certified copies of birth, death or marriage certificates and other vital records, the person requesting the certified copy should be referred to the appropriate Bureau of Vital Statistics. (See Bureaus of Vital Statistics, pages 108–112.)

Acknowledgments

A Common Notarial Act. Acknowledgments are one of the most common forms of notarization. Typically, they are executed on deeds and other documents affecting real property that will be publicly recorded by a County Recorder.

Purpose. In executing an acknowledgment, a Notary certifies three things: (Civil Code, Section 1885)

1) The signer *personally appeared* before the Notary on the date and in the state and county indicated on the notarial certificate (notarization cannot be based on a telephone call or on a Notary's familiarity with a signature); and

2) The signer was *positively identified* by the Notary through either personal knowledge or satisfactory evidence (see "Identifying Document Signers," pages 41–45); and

3) The signer *acknowledged* to the Notary that the signature was freely made for the purposes stated in the document. (If a document is willingly signed in the presence of the Notary, this tacit act can serve just as well as an oral statement of acknowledgment.)

Certificate for Acknowledgment. For every acknowledgment on a document that will be be filed in California, regardless of whom the signer is representing, a California Notary *must* fill out the following "all-purpose" certificate or closely similar wording: (Civil Code, Section 1189)

State of California   )
) ss.
County of _____)

On _____ (date) before me, _____ (name and title "Notary Public"), personally appeared _____ (name[s] of signer[s]), personally known to me (or proved to me on the basis of satisfactory evidence) to be the person(s) whose name(s) is/are subscribed to the within instrument and acknowledged to me that he/she/they executed the same in his/her/their authorized capacity(ies), and that by his/her/their signature(s) on the instrument the person(s), or the entity upon behalf of which the person(s) acted, executed the instrument.

WITNESS my hand and official seal.

_____ (Signature of Notary)   (Seal of Notary)

Any lawful acknowledgment form executed prior to January 1, 1993, when the above form became mandatory, will be honored. (Civil Code, Section 1189)

Certificate for Documents Filed Out of State. A California Notary may complete an acknowledgment certificate prescribed by or used in a U.S. state or jurisdiction other than California *only* if the document will be filed outside of California.

However, an out-of-state certificate may *not* be used if it requires the Notary to make any determination or certification not allowed by California law, such as certifying a signer's particular representative capacity as attorney in fact, corporate officer or other status. The out-of-state certificate may *refer* to the capacity claimed by the signer, but the Notary may not *certify* that the signer does, in fact, *have the authority* to sign under the claimed capacity. (Civil Code, Section 1189)

Identification of Acknowledger. In an acknowledgment, the Notary must identify the signer either through personal knowledge, credible identifying witness(es) or identification documents. (See "Identifying Document Signers," pages 41–45.) (Civil Code, Section 1185)

Witnessing Signature Not Required. For an acknowledgment, the document does *not* have to be signed in the Notary's presence; however, the signer must appear before the Notary at the time of notarization to *acknowledge having signed* the document.

A document may have been signed an hour before, a week

before, a year before, etc. — as long as the signer appears before the Notary with the signed document at the time of notarization to acknowledge that the signature is his or her own. (Conversely, for a jurat, requiring an oath or affirmation, the document must be signed in the presence of the Notary. See "Jurats," pages 34–36.)

Failure to Complete Acknowledgment. Failure to complete an acknowledgment at the same time the Notary's signature and seal are affixed to the document is reason for the Secretary of State to revoke, suspend or refuse to grant a Notary's commission. In addition, a fine of up to $750 may be imposed. (Government Code, Sections 8214.1 and 8214.15)

Out-of-State Acknowledgment. Acknowledgment certificates completed outside of California by Notaries of another state in accordance with the laws of that state may be recorded in California. (Civil Code, Section 1189)

Terminology. In discussing acknowledgments, it is important to use proper terms. A Notary *takes* or *executes* an acknowledgment, while a document signer *makes* or *gives* an acknowledgment.

Who May Take. Within the state, Notaries and the following officials may take acknowledgments and proofs in their jurisdictions: (Civil Code, Section 1181)

1) Clerks of superior, municipal and justice courts, of boards of supervisors, and of counties and cities;

2) Court commissioners; municipal, justice court and retired judges; county counsels; and

3) District and city attorneys.

Outside of California, but within the United States and jurisdictions, acknowledgments and proofs may be executed by: (Civil Code, Section 1182)

1) A Notary Public;

2) A judge, justice or clerk of any court of record of the United States;

3) A commissioner appointed by the Governor or Secretary of State; or

4) Any other authorized officer.

Outside of the United States, acknowledgments and proofs may be executed by: (Civil Code, Section 1183)

1) A Notary Public, providing the Notary's signature is proven before a judge of a court of record where the notarization is performed, or proven by any American diplomatic officer or authorized consular agent, or by *apostille*;

2) A judge of a court of record, or a consul, vice consul or consular agent of the United States in the foreign jurisdiction; or

3) A commissioner appointed by the Governor or Secretary of State.

Copies of Notarial Records

Public Request. A Notary must provide a photocopy — not a *certified copy* — of a journal line item entry if the request for the copy is in writing and includes the names of the persons whose signatures were notarized, the type of document, and the month and year of notarization. To protect the privacy of others, the Notary should cover adjacent entries when making the copy. A Notary may charge up to 30 cents per photocopy. (Government Code, Section 8206)

Employer Request. Effective January 1, 1998, an employer of a Notary may request inspection or copies of journal entries that are directly related to the employer's business if the inspection or copying is done in the Notary's presence. An employer may ask a Notary employee to regularly provide copies of business-related entries from the journal. The confidentiality and safekeeping of such journal copies are the employer's responsibility. The Notary shall *not* be required to allow inspection or provide copies of journal entries that are not related to the employer's business. (Government Code, Section 8206)

Regardless of whether it contains entries related to the business of the Notary's employer, the journal remains the exclusive property of the Notary and must not be surrendered to an employer upon termination of the Notary's employment. (Government Code, Section 8206)

Subpoena. A Notary must provide his or her notarial journal for examination and photocopying upon receipt of a subpoena duces tecum or court order. The copying must be performed in the presence of the Notary, and the Notary must certify the copies if requested. (Government Code, Section 8206)

Certified Copy. Within 30 days of receiving a written request from the Secretary of State, the Notary must furnish a *certified* copy of the requested journal entry. (Government Code, Section 8205)

Certificate for Certified Copy of Notarial Record. California law does not provide certificate wording for Notaries issuing certified copies of journal entries. The National Notary Association recommends the following form:

State of California   )
) ss.
County of _____)

On this the _____ day of _____ (month), _____ (year), I, _____ (name of Notary Public), the undersigned Notary Public, hereby declare that the attached reproduction of a Notary journal entry involving _____ (describe document, noting date and signer[s]) is a true and correct photocopy made from a page in my Notary journal.

_____ (Signature of Notary)   (Seal of Notary)

Certified Copies of Powers of Attorney

Procedure. In addition to notarizing signatures on powers of attorney, Notaries may certify copies of such documents. The Notary compares the copy to the original to verify that the copy is, in fact, identical to the original power of attorney document. Ideally, the Notary should personally make the photocopy that is to be certified to ensure that the copy is identical to the original. (Government Code, Section 8205 and Probate Code, Section 4307)

Certificate for Certified Copy of Power of Attorney. If certificate wording is not otherwise provided, the National Notary Association recommends the following wording for Notaries certifying copies of powers of attorney.

State of California   )
) ss.
County of _____)

On this the _____ day of _____ (month), _____ (year), I, _____ (name of Notary Public), the undersigned Notary Public, hereby certify that the attached document is a true, complete and unaltered photocopy of a power of attorney presented to me on this date by _____ (presenter's name), under Section 4307 of the California Probate Code.

_____ (Signature of Notary)   (Seal of Notary)

Journal Entry. As with all notarial acts, the Notary must complete a journal entry for a copy certification of a power of attorney document.

Identification of Presenter. Although not required by law, the Notary should properly identify the document presenter by the same identification standards prescribed for acknowledgments.

Copy Certification by Document Custodian

Purpose. Because California Notaries are *not* allowed to certify copies of any document except powers of attorney and journal records, copy certification by document custodian may often serve as an acceptable alternative when a Notary-certified copy (permitted in many other states and countries) is requested. Copy certification by document custodian may not be acceptable to the individual or agency receiving the copy, so the person requesting the act should verify that it will serve the required purposes.

Procedure. The permanent keeper of the document — the document custodian — certifies the copy, *not* the Notary. The custodian makes a photocopy of the original document; makes a written statement about the trueness, correctness and completeness of the copy; signs that statement before a Notary; and takes an oath or affirmation regarding the truth of the statement. The Notary, having witnessed the signing and given the oath or affirmation, executes a jurat.

Not for Vital Records. Copy certification by document custodian is not appropriate for vital records such as birth, marriage and death certificates, since originals of these documents are retained by public agencies. Persons requesting certified copies of vital records should be directed to the agency that holds the original — typically, the Bureau of Vital Statistics or County Clerk where the birth, death or marriage occurred.

<u>Certificate for Copy Certification by Document Custodian</u>. In addition to the jurat certificate, the custodian's statement is required. Although not prescribed by law, this wording — which includes the required jurat — is recommended by the National Notary Association:

> State of California)
>   ) ss.
> County of _____)
>
> I, _____ (name of custodian of original document), hereby swear (or affirm) that the attached reproduction of _____ (description of original document) is a true, correct and complete photocopy of a document in my possession.
>
> _____ (signature of custodian) _____ (address)
>
> Subscribed and sworn to (or affirmed) before me this _____ day of _____ (month), _____ (year), by _____ (name of custodian).
>
> _____ (Signature of Notary)   (Seal of Notary)

Depositions and Affidavits

<u>Purpose</u>. A deposition is a signed transcript of the signer's oral statements taken down for use in a judicial proceeding. This deposition signer is called the *deponent.*

An affidavit is a signed statement made under oath or affirmation by a person called an *affiant,* and it is used for a variety of purposes both in and out of court.

For both a deposition and an affidavit, the Notary must administer an oath or affirmation and complete some form of jurat, which the Notary signs and seals.

<u>Depositions</u>. With a deposition, both sides in a lawsuit or court case have the opportunity to cross-examine the deponent. Questions and answers are transcribed into a written statement. Used only in judicial proceedings, a deposition is then signed and sworn to before an oath-administering official.

California Notaries have the power to take depositions — meaning, to transcribe the words spoken aloud by a deponent —

but this duty is most often executed by trained and certified shorthand reporters, also known as court reporters.

Affidavits. Affidavits are used in and out of court for a variety of purposes, from declaring losses to an insurance company to declaring U.S. citizenship before traveling to a foreign country. An affidavit is a document containing a statement voluntarily signed and sworn to or affirmed before a Notary or other official with oath-administering powers. If used in a judicial proceeding, only one side in the case need participate in the execution of the affidavit, in contrast to the deposition.

In an affidavit, the Notary's certificate typically sandwiches the affiant's signed statement, with the venue and affiant's name at the top of the document and the jurat wording at the end. The Notary is responsible for the venue, affiant's name and any notarial text at the beginning and end of the affidavit, and the affiant is responsible for the signed statement in the middle.

Certificate for Depositions and Affidavits. Depositions and affidavits require jurat certificates. (See "Jurats," pages 34–36.)

Oath (Affirmation) for Depositions and Affidavits. If no other wording is prescribed in a given instance, a Notary may use the following language in administering an oath (or affirmation) for an affidavit or deposition:

> Do you solemnly swear that the statements made in this affidavit (or deposition) are the truth, the whole truth, and nothing but the truth, so help you God?

> (Do you solemnly affirm that the statements made in this affidavit [or deposition] are the truth, the whole truth, and nothing but the truth?)

Response Required. For an oath or affirmation, the affiant must respond aloud and affirmatively, with "I do" or "Yes" or the like.

Jurats

Part of Verification. In notarizing affidavits, depositions and other forms of written verification requiring an oath by the signer, the Notary normally executes a jurat.

Purpose. While the purpose of an acknowledgment is to positively identify a document signer, the purpose of a verification with jurat is to compel truthfulness by appealing to the signer's conscience and fear of criminal penalties for perjury. In executing a jurat, a Notary certifies that:

1) The signer *personally appeared* before the Notary at the time of notarization on the date and in the state and county indicated (notarization based on a telephone call or on familiarity with a signature is not acceptable); and

2) The Notary *watched the signature* being made at the time of notarization; and

3) The Notary *administered an oath* or affirmation to the signer.

Identification. Even though not required by law, the prudent Notary will also take pains to positively identify each signer (as is required by law for an acknowledgment).

Certificate for a Jurat. A typical jurat is the wording, "Subscribed and sworn to (or affirmed) before me..." or substantially similar language. California law prescribes the following jurat wording: (Civil Code, Section 1183.5)

State of California   )
) ss.
County of _____)

Subscribed and sworn to (or affirmed) before me on this _____ day of _____ (month), _____ (year).

_____ (Signature of Notary)   (Seal of Notary)

Verifying age. In executing a jurat on a document that includes the signer's date of birth or age and the signer's photograph or fingerprint, the Notary must verify the date of birth or age through a birth certificate or a state driver's license or nondriver's ID. (Government Code, Section 8230)

Wording for Jurat Oath (Affirmation). If not otherwise prescribed by law, a California Notary may use the following or similar words to administer an oath (or affirmation) in conjunction with a jurat:

Do you solemnly swear that the statements in this document are true to the best of your knowledge and belief, so help you God?

(Do you solemnly affirm that the statements in this document are true to the best of your knowledge and belief?)

Oath or Affirmation Not Administered. Failure to administer any oath or affirmation as required by law is reason for the Secretary of State to revoke, suspend or refuse to grant a Notary's commission. In addition, a fine of up to $750 may be imposed. (Government Code, Sections 8214.1 and 8214.15)

Oaths and Affirmations

Purpose. An oath is a solemn, spoken pledge to a Supreme Being. An affirmation is a solemn, spoken pledge on one's own personal honor, with no reference to a Supreme Being. Both are usually a promise of truthfulness, and have the same legal effect.

In taking an oath or affirmation in an official proceeding, a person may be subject to criminal penalties for perjury should he or she fail to be truthful.

An oath or affirmation can be a full-fledged notarial act in its own right, as when giving an oath of office to a public official (when "swearing in" a public official), or it can be part of the process of notarizing a document (e.g., executing a jurat, swearing in a subscribing witness).

A person who objects to taking an oath — pledging to a Supreme Being — may instead be given an affirmation, which does not refer to a Supreme Being.

Power to Administer. California Notaries and certain other officers are authorized to administer oaths and affirmations. (Code of Civil Procedure, Section 2093)

Wording for Oath (Affirmation). If law does not dictate otherwise, a California Notary may use the following or similar words in administering an oath (or affirmation):

- Oath (Affirmation) for an affiant signing an affidavit:

Do you solemnly swear that the statements in this document are true to the best of your knowledge and belief, so help you God?

(Do you solemnly affirm that the statements in this document are true to the best of your knowledge and belief?)

- Oath (Affirmation) for a witness testifying in a court case: (California Code of Civil Procedure, Section 2094)

Do you solemnly swear that the evidence you shall give in this issue (or matter), pending between (first party) and (second party), shall be the truth, the whole truth, and nothing but the truth, so help you God?

(Do you solemnly affirm that the evidence you shall give in this issue [or matter], pending between [first party] and [second party], shall be the truth, the whole truth, and nothing but the truth?)

- Oath (Affirmation) for a credible identifying witness: (Civil Code, Section 1185)

Do you solemnly swear that (person making the acknowledgment) is the person named in the document; that (person making the acknowledgment) is personally known to you; that it is your reasonable belief that the circumstances of (person making the acknowledgment) are such that it would be very difficult or impossible for him/her to obtain another form of identification; that (person making the acknowledgment) does not possess any of the acceptable identification documents; and that you do not have a financial interest nor are you named in the document being acknowledged, so help you God?

(Do you solemnly affirm that [person making the acknowledgment] is the person named in the document; that [person making the acknowledgment] is personally known to you; that it is your reasonable belief that the circumstances of [person making the acknowledgment] are such that it would be very difficult or impossible for him/her to obtain another form of identification; that [person making the acknowledgment] does not possess any of the acceptable identification documents; and that you do not have a financial interest nor are you named in the document being acknowledged?)

- Oath (Affirmation) for a subscribing witness:

Do you solemnly swear that you saw (name of the document signer) sign his/her name to this document and/or that he/she acknowledged to you having executed it for the purposes therein stated, so help you God?

(Do you solemnly affirm that you saw [name of the document signer] sign his/her name to this document and/or that he/she acknowledged to you having executed it for the purposes therein stated?)

Response Required. The oath or affirmation wording must be spoken aloud, and the person taking the oath or affirmation must answer affirmatively with, "I do," "Yes," or the like. A nod or grunt is not a clear and sufficient response. If a person is unable to speak, the Notary may rely on written notes to communicate.

Ceremony and Gestures. To impress upon the oath-taker or affirmant the importance of truthfulness, the Notary is encouraged to lend a sense of ceremony and formality to the oath or affirmation. During administration of an oath or affirmation, the Notary and document signer may raise their right hands, though this is not a legal requirement. Notaries generally have discretion to use words and gestures they feel will most compellingly appeal to the conscience of the oath-taker or affirmant.

Oath or Affirmation Not Administered. Failure to administer any oath or affirmation as required by law is reason for the Secretary of State to revoke, suspend or refuse to grant a Notary's commission. In addition, a fine of up to $750 may be imposed. (Government Code, Sections 8214.1 and 8214.15)

Proof of Execution by Subscribing Witness

Purpose. In executing a proof of execution, a Notary certifies that the signature of a person who does not appear before the Notary — the principal signer — is genuine and freely made based on the sworn testimony of another person who does appear — a subscribing (signing) witness.

Proofs of execution are used when the principal signer is out of town or otherwise unavailable to appear before a Notary. Because of their high potential for fraudulent abuse, proofs should only be used as a last resort and never merely because the principal signer prefers not to take the time to personally appear before a Notary.

In Lieu of Acknowledgment. On recordable documents, a proof of execution is usually regarded as an acceptable substitute for an acknowledgement. (Civil Code, Section 1195)

Limitations. Proofs of execution are not permitted with mortgages, deeds of trust, security agreements, quitclaim deeds and grant deeds, but are allowed with trustee's deeds resulting from foreclosure and deeds of reconveyance. (Government Code, Section 27287 and Civil Code, Section 1195)

Subscribing Witness. A subscribing witness is a person who watches a principal sign a document (or who personally takes the principal's acknowledgment) and then subscribes (signs) his or her own name on the document at the principal's request. This witness brings that document to a Notary on the principal's behalf and takes an oath or affirmation from the Notary to the effect that the principal did willingly sign (or acknowledge signing) the document and requested the witness to also sign the document.

The ideal subscribing witness personally knows the principal signer and has no beneficial interest in the document or transaction. It would be foolish of the Notary, for example, to rely on the word of a subscribing witness presenting for notarization a power of attorney that names this very witness as attorney in fact.

Oath (Affirmation) for a Subscribing Witness. An acceptable oath for the subscribing witness might be:

> Do you solemnly swear that you saw (name of the document signer) sign his/her name to this document and/or that he/she acknowledged to you having executed it for the purposes therein stated, so help you God?

> (Do you solemnly affirm that you saw [name of the document signer] sign his/her name to this document and/or that he/she acknowledged to you having executed it for the purposes therein stated?)

The subscribing witness then signs the Notary's journal and the Notary completes a proof of execution by subscribing witness certificate, often called a *witness jurat.*

Identifying Subscribing Witness. The subscribing witness *must* be personally known to the Notary, or the identity must be proved on the oath of one credible identifying witness who is personally known to the Notary. (Civil Code, Section 1196)

Certificate for Proof of Execution. Effective January 1, 1998, California law prescribes a certificate for a proof of execution by a subscribing witness. Other certificates may also be used as long as they substantially comply with the required wording. (Civil Code, Section 1195)

> State of California   )
>   ) ss.
> County of _____)

> On _____ (date), before me, the undersigned, a Notary Public for the state, personally appeared _____ (subscribing witness's name), personally known to me (or proved to me on the oath of _____ [credible identifying witness's name], who is personally known to me) to be the person whose name is subscribed to the within

instrument, as a witness thereto, who, being by me duly sworn, deposed and said that he/she was present and saw _____ (name[s] of principal[s]), the same person(s) described in and whose name(s) is/are subscribed to the within and annexed instrument in his/her/their authorized capacity(ies) as (a) party(ies) thereto, execute the same, and that said affiant subscribed his/her name to the within instrument as a witness at the request of _____ (name[s] of principal[s]).

WITNESS my hand and official seal.

_____ (Signature of Notary)   (Seal of Notary)

Do Not Use All-Purpose Acknowledgement Form. The so-called "all-purpose" acknowledgment certificate, prescribed in Civil Code Section 1189, should *not* be used for proofs of execution. California recorders will likely reject documents with all-purpose acknowledgment certificates used or adapted in place of proofs.

Protests

Purpose. In rare instances, Notaries may be asked to protest a negotiable instrument for nonpayment. A protest is a written statement by a Notary or other authorized officer verifying that payment was not received on an instrument such as a bank draft. Failure to pay is called *dishonor.* Before issuing a certificate of protest, the Notary must present the bank draft or other instrument to the person or entity obliged to pay, a procedure called *presentment.* (Uniform Commercial Code, Section 3505)

Antiquated Act. In the 19th century, protests were common notarial acts in the United States, but they rarely are performed today due to the advent of modern electronic communications and resulting changes in our banking and financial systems. Modern Notaries most often encounter protests in the context of international commerce.

Special Knowledge Required. Notarial acts of protest are complicated and varied, requiring a special knowledge of financial and legal terminology. Only Notaries who have the requisite special knowledge, or who are acting under the supervision of an experienced bank officer or an attorney familiar with the Uniform Commercial Code, should attempt a protest.

Certificate for Protest. When a Notary protests a promissory note or bill for nonpayment or nonacceptance, the protest certificate must include the following: (Government Code, Section 8208)

1) The time and place of presentment of the bill or note;

2) That presentment was made and how presentment was made;

3) The cause or reason for protesting the bill; and

4) The demand made and the answer given, if any, or the fact that the drawee or acceptor could not be found.

Protests from Out of State. When protesting bills of exchange or notes, a California Notary may exercise any additional customary powers and duties prescribed by the other state or nation for that protest. This authorization applies only to protests and not any other notarial act. (Government Code, Section 8205)

PRACTICES AND PROCEDURES

Identifying Document Signers

Acknowledgments. In taking acknowledgments for any document, California law requires the Notary to identify the acknowledger. The following three methods of identification are acceptable: (Civil Code, Section 1185)

1) The Notary's *personal knowledge* of the signer's identity (See "Personal Knowledge of Identity," page 42);

2) The oath or affirmation of one personally known *credible identifying witness* or two *credible identifying witnesses* identified by authorized ID documents (See "Credible Identifying Witnesses," pages 42–44); or

3) Reliable *identification documents* or ID cards (See "Identification Documents," pages 44–45).

Identification for Other Notarial Acts. While the law specifies identification standards only for acknowledgers, the prudent and conscientious Notary will apply these same standards in identifying any signer, whether for an acknowledgment, jurat or any other notarial act.

Verifying Representative Capacity. The California Notary is not required nor authorized to verify the capacity in which a person signs — such as corporate officer, trustee, partner to a partnership, attorney in fact, or other representative capacity. The Notary only identifies the acknowledging signer as an individual. (Civil Code, Section 1185)

Personal Knowledge of Identity

Definition. The safest and most reliable method of identifying a document signer is for the Notary to depend on his or her own personal knowledge of the signer's identity. Personal knowledge means familiarity with an individual resulting from interactions with that person over a period of time sufficient to eliminate every reasonable doubt that the person has the identity claimed. The familiarity should come from association with the individual in relation to other people and should be based upon a chain of circumstances surrounding the individual.

California law does not specify how long a Notary must be acquainted with an individual before personal knowledge of identity may be claimed. The Notary's common sense must prevail. In general, the longer the Notary is acquainted with a person, and the more interactions the Notary has had with that person, the more likely the individual is indeed personally known.

For instance, the Notary might safely regard a friend since childhood as personally known, but would be foolish to consider a person met for the first time the previous day as such. Whenever the Notary has a reasonable doubt about a signer's identity, that individual should be considered not personally known, and the identification should be made through either a credible identifying witness or reliable identification documents.

Credible Identifying Witness(es)

Purpose. When a document signer is not personally known to the Notary and is not able to present reliable ID cards, that signer may be identified on the oath (or affirmation) of one or two credible identifying witness(es). (Civil Code, Section 1185)

Qualifications. Every credible identifying witness must personally know the document signer. If there is only one credible identifying witness to identify the signer, that witness must be personally known by the Notary. If there are two credible identifying witnesses available to identify the signer, these witnesses may be identified through an identification document listed under "Identification Documents," pages 44–45.

A credible identifying witness must not have an interest or be named in the document. A credible identifying witness must know that the signer has no identification and that it would be impractical to obtain the necessary ID. (Civil Code, Section 1185)

Oath (Affirmation) for Credible Identifying Witness. To ensure truthfulness, the Notary must administer an oath or affirmation to each credible identifying witness. The credible identifying witness must swear or affirm that the following are true: (Civil Code, Section 1185)

1) The person making the acknowledgment is the person named in the document; and

2) The person making the acknowledgment is personally known to the witness; and

3) That it is the reasonable belief of the witness that it is very difficult or impossible for the person making the acknowledgment to obtain another form of identification; and

4) The person making the acknowledgment does not possess any of the acceptable identification documents; and

5) The witness does not have a financial interest in the document and is not named in the document.

An acceptable oath (affirmation) for a credible identifying witness might be:

Do you solemnly swear that (person making the acknowledgment) is the person named in the document; that (person making the acknowledgment) is personally known to you; that it is your reasonable belief that the circumstances of (person making the acknowledgment) are such that it would be very difficult or impossible for him/her to obtain another form of identification; that (person making the acknowledgment) does not possess any of the acceptable identification documents; and that you do not have a financial interest nor are you named in the document being acknowledged, so help you God?

(Do you solemnly affirm that [person making the acknowledgment] is the person named in the document; that [person making the acknowledgment] is personally known to you; that it is your reasonable belief that the circumstances of [person making the acknowledgment] are such that it would be very difficult or impossible for him/her to obtain another form of identification; that [person making the acknowledgment] does not possess any of the acceptable identification documents; and that you do not have a financial interest nor are you named in the document being acknowledged?)

Signature in Notary's Journal. Each credible identifying witness must sign the Notary's journal, along with the document signer. The Notary must indicate how the credible identifying witness was identified, either by the Notary's personal knowledge (required for one credible identifying witness) or through current identification documents (two credible identifying witnesses are then necessary).

Indicate on Certificate. To indicate reliance on a credible identifying witness or witnesses, the Notary should select the phrase "proved to me on the basis of satisfactory evidence" that appears in the California all-purpose acknowledgment certificate.

Not a Subscribing Witness. Do not confuse *credible identifying* witnesses with *subscribing* witnesses. A credible identifying witness vouches for the identity of a signer who appears before the Notary. A subscribing witness vouches for the genuineness of the signature of a person who does not appear before the Notary. (See "Proof of Execution by Subscribing Witness," pages 38–40.)

Identification Documents (ID Cards)

Acceptable Identification Documents. A Notary may identify a document signer through any one of the identification documents listed below. The document must 1) be current or, if expired, issued within the past five years, 2) contain the document signer's photograph, personal description, and signature; and 3) bear a serial or other identifying number: (Civil Code, Section 1185)

- California driver's license or nondriver's ID issued by the California Department of Motor Vehicles. (If accompanied by a current extension card, a driver's license issued more than five years ago is acceptable.)

- U.S. passport (physical description not required).

- Foreign passport stamped by the U.S. Immigration and

Naturalization Service (INS).

- Driver's license or nondriver's ID issued by another U.S. state.

- Driver's license officially issued in Mexico or Canada.

- U.S. military ID.

- Inmate ID issued by the California Department of Corrections (but *only* to identify prisoners in custody).

- Resident alien ID, or "green card," issued by the Immigration and Naturalization Service (INS), but *only* for notarization of INS forms. (Government Code, Section 8230)

Unacceptable Identification Documents. Identification documents that are not acceptable for identifying acknowledgers include Social Security cards, credit cards, temporary driver's licenses and driver's licenses without photographs.

Multiple Identification. While one good identification document or card may be sufficient to identify a signer, the Notary may ask for more.

Journal of Notarial Acts

Requirement. California Notaries are required to keep one active sequential journal of all their official acts. A permanently bound recordbook (not loose-leaf) with numbered pages and entry spaces is best for preserving the sequence of notarial acts and for protecting against unauthorized removal of pages or tampering. (Government Code, Section 8206)

Security of Journal. Effective January 1, 1998, the journal must be kept in a locked and secured area under direct supervision and control of the Notary. (Government Code, Section 8206)
Failure to secure the journal is reason for the Secretary of State to revoke, suspend or refuse to grant a Notary's commission. In addition, a fine of up to $750 may be imposed. (Government Code, Sections 8214.1 and 8214.15)

Failure to Keep. Failure to keep a journal of notarial acts is reason for the Secretary of State to revoke, suspend or refuse to grant a Notary's commission. In addition, a fine may be imposed. (Government Code, Sections 8214.1 and 8214.15)

Journal Entries. For each notarization, the journal must contain the following entries: (Government Code, Section 8206)

1) The date, time of day, and type of notarization (e.g., jurat, acknowledgment, etc.);

2) The type of document notarized (e.g., deed of trust, affidavit of support, etc.);

3) The signature of each person whose signature is notarized, including the signature of any subscribing witness;

4) A statement as to how the signer's identity was confirmed (If by personal knowledge, the journal entry should read "Personal Knowledge." If by satisfactory evidence, the journal entry must contain either: a description of the ID card accepted, including the type of ID, the government agency issuing the ID, the serial or identifying number, and the date of issuance or expiration; or the signature[s] of the credible identifying witness[es] and how the credible identifying witness[es] was [were] identified — see "Credible Identifying Witness(es)," pages 42–44);

5) The fee charged for the notarial service; and

6) For deeds, quitclaim deeds and deeds of trust affecting any real property, the right thumbprint of each signer or subscribing witness. (See below.)

Journal Thumbprint Requirement. *All* signers of deeds, quitclaim deeds and deeds of trust affecting *any* real property must leave a right thumbprint in the Notary's journal of notarial acts. Exempted from the journal print requirement are deeds of reconveyance and trustee's deeds resulting from a decree of foreclosure or a nonjudicial foreclosure. (Government Code, Section 8206)

If the signer's right thumbprint is not available, the Notary is required to obtain the left thumbprint or a print of any available finger. The Notary must note this in the journal. If the signer is physically unable to leave a thumbprint or a fingerprint, the Notary must note this in the journal with an explanation of the signer's physical condition. (Government Code, Section 8206)

The journal thumbprint is a strong deterrent to forgery, because it represents absolute proof of the forger's identity. Nothing prevents a Notary from asking for a thumbprint for every notarial act, if the signer is willing. It can only be made a precondition for notarizing when the document is a deed affecting real estate.

Journal-Entry Copies. A Notary's journal is a public record. Accordingly, if any member of the public submits a written request specifying the month and year of a particular notarization, as well as the type of document and the names of the signers, the Notary must provide that person with a photocopy of the particular entry in the journal — but of no other entries! Adjacent entries should be covered by a sheet of blank paper. The Notary may charge no more than 30 cents per photocopy. (Government Code, Section 8206) (See "Copies of Notarial Records," pages 30–31.)

The state discourages "fishing expeditions" through the Notary journal by persons who are not able to be specific about the entry sought.

Employer Request. Effective January 1, 1998, an employer of a Notary may request inspection or copies of journal entries that are directly related to the employer's business if the inspection or copying is done in the Notary's presence. An employer may ask a Notary employee to regularly provide copies of business-related entries from the journal. The confidentiality and safekeeping of such journal copies are the employer's responsibility. The Notary shall *not* be required to allow inspection or provide copies of journal entries that are not related to the employer's business. (Government Code, Section 8206)

Never Surrender Journal. Notaries should never surrender control of their official journals to anyone, unless expressly subpoenaed by a court order or demanded by a peace officer. Even when an employer has paid for the Notary's official journal and seal — and regardless of whether the journal contains entries related to the employer's business — they go with the Notary upon termination of employment; no person but the Notary can lawfully possess and use these official adjuncts of office. (Government Code, Section 8206)

Lost or Stolen Journal. A Notary must *immediately* notify the

Secretary of State by certified or registered mail if a journal is lost, stolen, misplaced, destroyed, damaged, or otherwise rendered unusable. In the notification, the Notary must include his or her commission number and expiration date, the time period covered by the journal entries, and a photocopy of any relevant police report. (Government Code, Section 8206)

Destruction of Notary Records. It is a misdemeanor for any person to purposely destroy, deface or conceal a Notary's journal. A person who does so is liable for damages suffered by any person as a result. (Government Code, Sections 8209 and 8221)

Disposal of Notary Records. If a Notary resigns, is disqualified, is removed from office or allows a commission to expire without obtaining another commission within 30 days, then his or her notarial records must be delivered to the County Clerk's office where the Notary's oath of office and bond are on file within 30 days of commission resignation, revocation or expiration.

If a Notary refuses to deliver notarial records to the County Clerk as specified by law, the Notary is guilty of a misdemeanor and is liable for damages suffered by any person as a result.

If the Notary dies, the Notary's executor or personal representative must promptly notify the Secretary of State and deliver all the deceased's notarial records and papers to the County Clerk's office where the Notary's oath and bond are filed.

After 10 years, the office of the County Clerk may destroy the notarial records upon court order. Notaries may never destroy their notarial records. (Government Code, Section 8209)

Answer Inquiries from State. Upon official request, a Notary must send certified copies of journal entries to the Secretary of State. The Notary must respond within 30 days to the Secretary of State's request, sent by certified mail, for information relating to official acts performed by the Notary. (Government Code, Section 8205) (See "Copies of Notarial Records," pages 30–31.)

Notarial Certificate

Requirement. In notarizing any document, a Notary must complete a notarial certificate. The certificate is wording that indicates exactly what the Notary has certified. The notarial certificate may either be printed on the document itself or on an attachment to it. The certificate should contain:

1) A *venue* indicating where the notarization is performed. "State of California, County of _____," is the typical venue wording, with the county name inserted in the blank. The letters "SS." or "SCT." sometimes appear after the venue; they abbreviate the traditional Latin word *scilicet*, meaning "in particular" or "namely."

2) A *statement of particulars* indicating what the notarization has attested to. An acknowledgment certificate would include such wording as: "On _____ (date) before me, _____ (name of Notary), personally appeared, _____ (name of signer), personally known to me (or proved to me on the basis of satisfactory evidence) to be the person(s)...." A jurat certificate would include such wording as: "Subscribed and sworn to (or affirmed) before me this _____ (date)...."

3) A *testimonium clause*, which may be optional if the date is included in the statement of particulars: "Witness my hand and official seal, this the _____ day of _____ (month), ____ (year)." In this short sentence, the Notary formally attests to the truthfulness of the preceding facts in the certificate. "Hand" means signature.

4) The *official signature of the Notary*, exactly as the name appears on the Notary's commissioning paper.

5) The *official seal of the Notary*. On many certificates the letters "L.S." appear, indicating where the seal is to be located. These letters abbreviate the Latin term *locus sigilli*, meaning "place of the seal." An inking seal should be placed near but not over the letters, so that wording imprinted by the seal will not be obscured. An embossing seal, used in conjunction with an inking seal, may be placed directly over the letters — slightly displacing portions of the characters and leaving a clue that document examiners can use to distinguish an original from a forged photocopy.

Loose Certificates. When certificate wording is not preprinted on the document, a "loose" certificate may be attached by the Notary. This form is typically stapled to the document's left margin following the signature page. Only one side of the certificate should be stapled, so it can be lifted to view the document.

To prevent a loose certificate from being removed and fraudulently placed on another document, there are precautions a Notary can take. The Notary can emboss the certificate and document together, writing, "Attached document bears embossment," on the certificate. Or the Notary can write a brief description of the document on the certificate: e.g., "This certificate is attached to a _____ (title or type of document), dated _____, of _____ (number) pages, also signed by _____ (name[s] of other signer[s])."

While fraud-deterrent steps such as these can make it much more difficult for a loose certificate to be removed and misused, there is no absolute protection against its removal and misuse. Notaries must absolutely ensure that while a certificate remains in their control, it is attached only to its intended document.

Do Not Pre-Sign/Seal Certificates. A Notary should *never* sign and/or seal certificates ahead of time or permit other persons to attach loose notarial certificates to documents. Nor should the Notary send an unattached, signed and sealed, loose certificate through the mail, even if requested to do so by a signer who previously appeared before the Notary. These actions may facilitate fraud or forgery, and they could subject the Notary to lawsuits to recover damages resulting from the Notary's neglect or misconduct. In addition, the Secretary of State could fine the Notary up to $750 and revoke, suspend or refuse to renew the Notary's commission. (Government Code, Section 8214.1)

Standard Size for Certificates. Additional recording fees will be charged for documents when *any* page of the document, including the attached notarial certificate, is not the standard 8½ by 11-inch size. The extra fee is $3 per page and is applied to all pages of the document. The person who files the document is responsible for the extra fees, not the Notary. (Government Code, Sections 27361 and 27361.5)

False Certificate. A Notary who knowingly completes a false notarial certificate is guilty of a misdemeanor and subject to criminal penalties. Further, the Notary may have his or her commission suspended or revoked and be fined up to $1,500. A Notary would be completing a false certificate, for example, if he or she signed and sealed an acknowledgment certificate indicating a signer personally appeared when the signer actually did not. (Government Code, Sections 6203, 8214.1 and 8214.15)

Notary Seal

Requirement. A California Notary must affix an impression of an official seal on the certificate portion of every document notarized. (Government Code, Section 8207)

Format. The seal may either be circular, not more than two inches in diameter, or rectangular, not more than an inch in height and two and one-half inches in length. It must have a serrated or milled edged border. (Government Code, Section 8207)

Inking and Embosser Seals. The seal must imprint or emboss a photographically reproducible impression. Because the image must be photocopiable, most Notaries use an inked rubber stamp seal, since an embossment would have to be smudged or darkened to be picked up by a camera. An embosser may be used in addition to the required photographically reproducible seal, but it must not be used over the reproducible inking seal nor over the Notary's signature. (Government Code, Section 8207)

Required Information. The seal impression must clearly show the following information: (Government Code, Section 8207)

- Name of the Notary (exactly as it appears on the commission certificate);

- The circular California state seal;

- The words "Notary Public";

- The county where the Notary's oath and bond are filed;

- The Notary's commission expiration date;

- The Notary's commission number; and

- The ID number of the seal manufacturer or vendor.

Lost or Damaged Seal. Any Notary whose official seal is lost, misplaced, destroyed, broken, damaged or otherwise unworkable must immediately mail or deliver written notice to the Secretary of State, who will issue a Certificate of Authorization to obtain a replacement. Failure to report can result in a $1,500 fine. (Government Code, Section 8207.3)

Security of Seal. Effective January 1, 1998, the seal must be kept in a locked and secured area under direct supervision and control of the Notary. Failure to secure the seal is reason for the Secretary of State to revoke, suspend or refuse to grant a Notary commission. In addition, a fine of up to $750 may be imposed. (Government Code, Sections 8207, 8214.1 and 8214.15)

Certificate of Authorization. No person may purchase a California Notary seal without first presenting to the seal vendor a Certificate of Authorization to Purchase a Notary Stamp, issued by the Secretary of State. This certificate is sent to each newly commissioned Notary, along with the commissioning paper. (Government Code, Sections 8207.2)

The seal vendor must keep a copy of each Certificate of Authorization presented and a record of each Notary's ID number. The original Certificate of Authorization, containing a sample impression of the new seal, must be submitted to the Secretary of State for verification of the vendor's authority to manufacture a seal and for recordkeeping. (Government Code, Sections 8207.3)

The failure of a Notary or vendor to comply with these procedures regarding the Certificate of Authorization can result in a $1,500 fine for each violation. Such a penalty would result from a civil lawsuit initiated by the state attorney general or a local district attorney, city attorney or prosecutor. (Government Code, Sections 8207.4)

Misuse of Seal. Any person who, with intent to defraud, forges or counterfeits a Notary seal to give a document the appearance of being government-issued is guilty of forgery. Documents may include, but are not limited to, an identification card, driver's license, birth certificate, passport or Social Security card. In addition, forgery is punishable by imprisonment for up to one year. (Penal Code, Sections 472 and 473)

Use of Seal for Endorsement or Testimonial. Notaries may not use the official seal to endorse or promote any product, service or contest. The Notary seal may only be used to carry out the official duties of a Notary Public. (Government Code, Section 8207)

Placement of Seal Impression. The Notary's official seal impression should be placed near the Notary's signature on the notarial certificate. It must be easily readable and should not be placed over signatures or any printed matter on the document. An illegible or improperly placed seal may result in rejection of the document by a recorder.

L.S. The letters "L.S." — from the Latin *locus sigilli*, meaning "location of the seal" — appear on many notarial certificates to indicate where the Notary seal should be placed. Only an embosser seal, used in addition to an inking seal, should be placed *over* these letters. The inking seal should be placed *near* but not over the letters.

Plastic Subdivision Maps. Because many seal inks smear on plastic-surfaced subdivision maps, acknowledgment certificates printed on such maps need not bear the Notary's seal if the Notary's name, county of principal place of business, and commission expiration date are typed or printed below the Notary's signature. (Government Code, Section 66436)

Fees for Notarial Services

Maximum Fees. The following maximum fees are authorized for California Notaries:

- Acknowledgments — $10. For taking an acknowledgment, the fee is not to exceed $10 for each signature — that is, the acknowledger's signature, not the Notary's. For notarizing a single document with signatures of three persons appearing before the Notary, for example, a maximum of $30 could be charged. (Government Code, Section 8211)

- Certified Copy of Power of Attorney — $10. A maximum of $10 per copy may be charged by a Notary for certifying a copy of a power of attorney. (Government Code, Section 8211)

- Copy of Journal Entry — 30¢. A maximum of 30 cents per photocopy may be charged for providing a photocopy of an entry in the Notary's journal. (Government Code, Section 8206)

- Depositions — $20. For all services rendered in taking a deposition, the maximum fee is $20, plus $5 for administering an oath to the witness and $5 for completing the certificate on the deposition. (Government Code, Section 8211)

- Immigration Papers — $10 per set. A nonattorney Notary bonded as an immigration consultant may not charge more than $10 per set of forms (apart from the standard notarial fee) for entering data provided by a client on state or federal immigration forms. Violators may be fined up to $750. (Government Code, Sections 8214.1, 8214.15 and 8223)

- Jurats — $10. For executing a jurat, including the administration of the oath or affirmation, the fee is not to exceed $10 per person. (Government Code, Section 8211)

- Oaths and Affirmations — $10. For administering an oath or affirmation, with or without completion of a jurat, the fee is not to exceed $10 per person. (Government Code, Section 8211)

- Proofs of Execution by Subscribing Witness — $10. For taking a proof of execution, the maximum fee is the same as for an acknowledgment, $10 for each signature of the principal proven by a subscribing witness. (Government Code, Section 8211)

- Protests — $10. For taking a protest, the maximum fee is $10. For serving a notice of nonpayment or nonacceptance, the fee is $5. For recording every protest, the fee is $5. (Government Code, Section 8211)

Option Not to Charge. Notaries are not required to charge for their notarial services, and they may charge any fee less than the maximum. However, Notaries employed by some public agencies may be required by their employers to charge for their services and to remit the fees to the employer. (Government Code, Section 6100)

Overcharging. Charging more than the legally prescribed fees is reason for the Secretary of State to revoke, suspend or refuse to grant a Notary's commission. In addition, a fine of up to $750 may be imposed. (Government Code, Sections 8214.1 and 8214.15)

Travel Fees. Charges for travel by a Notary are not specified by law. Such fees are allowed only if Notary and signer agree beforehand on the amount to be charged. The signer must understand that a travel fee is not stipulated in law and is separate from the notarial fees described above.

Obligation to Itemize. A Notary employed by a county or judicial district is required to make out a receipt for notarial fees for any person requesting one. The Notary is liable for three times the notarial fee for neglecting or refusing to honor such a request. (Government Code, Section 6109)

Failure to Complete Notarization. For failing or refusing to complete a lawful request for notarization once payment is offered for it, a Notary is liable for any resulting ramifications. (Government Code, Section 6110)

Notary/Employer Agreement. A private employer who purchases the notarial supplies and bond of an employee Notary may make a voluntarily mutual agreement with the employee Notary to remit all notarial fees collected to the fund from which the employee Notary is paid. (Government Code, Section 8202.7)

No Fees Allowed for Election Papers. No fee may be charged to notarize signatures on absentee ballot identification envelopes or other voting materials. (Government Code, Section 8211)

A Notary is also prohibited from charging fees for notarizing any nomination document or circulator's affidavit. (Elections Code, Section 8080)

Incomplete Documents

Do Not Notarize. California Notaries are specifically prohibited from taking an acknowledgment or a proof of execution of any document that is not complete. (Government Code, Section 8205)

Any blanks in a document should be filled in by the signer. If the blanks are inapplicable and intended to be left unfilled, the signer should be asked to line through each space (using ink) or to write "Not Applicable" or "NA."

If there is doubt about a document's completeness, the Notary should ask the signer. If the signer says the instrument is incomplete, the Notary should refuse to notarize; if the signer says it is complete, the Notary might accept the signer's word, unless the document contains obvious blanks.

Disqualifying Interest

Financial or Beneficial Interest. A Notary may not perform any notarization related to a transaction in which that Notary has a direct financial or beneficial interest. (Government Code, Section 8224)

A financial or beneficial interest exists when the Notary is individually named as a principal in a financial transaction or when the Notary receives an advantage, right, privilege, property, or fee valued in excess of the lawfully prescribed notarial fee.

In regard to real estate transactions, a Notary is considered to have a disqualifying financial or beneficial interest when that Notary is a grantor or grantee, a mortgagor or mortgagee, a trustor or trustee, a vendor or vendee, a lessor or lessee, or a beneficiary in any way of the transaction.

Exemptions. Certain persons are exempt from this beneficial and financial interest provision. A Notary who is an agent, employee, insurer, attorney, escrow officer or lender for a person signing a document may notarize the document without being considered to have a disqualifying interest. For example, a real estate agent can notarize a document relating to a property transfer even if the agent derives a commission from that transaction.

Any challenged case of disqualifying financial or beneficial interest would be decided in court on its own merits. Thus, it is always safest for a Notary to ensure that he or she has no financial or beneficial interest whatsoever in a transaction regardless of what the law allows. (Government Code, Section 8224)

Refusal of Services

Legal Requests for Services. Notaries must honor all lawful and reasonable requests to notarize, whether or not the person requesting the act is a client or customer of the Notary or the Notary's employer. Not providing services when required to do so could cause the Notary to be liable if any damages resulted from the refusal. (Government Code, Section 6110)

Exception for Employer/Notary Agreement. A Notary and employer may agree to limit the Notary's services solely to transactions directly related to the employer's business. (See "Employer/Notary Agreement," pages 57–58.) (Government Code, Section 8202.8)

Reasonable Care

Responsibility. As public servants, Notaries must act responsibly and exercise reasonable care in the performance of their official duties. If a Notary fails to do so, he or she may be subject to a civil suit to recover financial damages caused by the Notary's error or omission. In general, reasonable care is a degree of concern and attentiveness that a person of normal intelligence and responsibility would exhibit. If a Notary can show to a judge or jury that he or she did everything expected of a reasonable person, the judge or jury is obligated by law to find the Notary blameless and not liable for damages.

Complying with all pertinent laws is the first rule of reasonable care for a Notary. And, if there are no statutory guidelines in a given instance, the Notary should "bend over backwards" to use common sense and prudence. (See "Steps to Proper Notarization," pages 14–17.)

Employer/Notary Agreement

Agreement to Limit Notary's Services. A private employer who has paid for an employee Notary's commissioning fees and for the notarial bond, stamp and other supplies *may* limit the Notary's services during business hours solely to transactions directly related to the employer's business, *if* the Notary agrees. (Government Code, Sections 8202.7 and 8202.8)

It may be helpful to the Notary to have this agreement in writing to prevent any haggling when limiting services.

Noncustomer Discrimination Prohibited. An employer/Notary agreement does not permit discrimination between customers and noncustomers, but only between *business-related* and *nonbusiness-related* documents. A business-related document is one that the employer is either named in or acting as an agent in relation to. If a bank customer asks an employee Notary, who has entered into such an agreement with the bank, to notarize a document that does not involve the bank, the Notary must refuse. (Government Code, Section 8202.8)

Once a Notary enters into an agreement with an employer to notarize business-related documents only, the Notary may not suspend the agreement just for customers or even for colleagues, coworkers or supervisors. However, the Notary may notarize other types of documents during nonbusiness hours. (Government Code, Section 8202.7)

Fees. A Notary who enters into such an agreement with a private employer *may* agree to hand over the notarial fees to the employer. The law requires the employer to place these fees into the account from which the Notary is paid.

Not Applicable to Government Employees. Employer/Notary agreements do not apply to government-employee Notaries.

Signature by Mark

Mark Serves as Signature. A person who cannot sign his or her name because of illiteracy or disability may instead use a mark — an "X" for example — as a signature, as long as there are two witnesses to the making of the mark. (Civil Code, Section 14)

Witnesses. For a mark to be notarized, two witnesses to the making of the mark are recommended in addition to the Notary. Both witnesses should sign the document and the Notary's journal. One witness should print legibly the marker's name beside the mark on the document, and also in the journal. (Civil Code, Section 14)

Witnesses' Statement. For a document to be filed in California, County Recorders require the witnesses to sign a statement on the document confirming the particulars of the procedure. This statement is in addition to the notarial certificate. California County Recorders prefer the following wording:

> _____ (name of signer), being unable to write, made his/her mark in our presence and requested the first of the undersigned to write his/her name, which he/she did, and we now subscribe our names as witnesses thereto.
>
> _____ (Signature of witness #1)
> _____ (Signature of witness #2)

Signature-by-Mark Certificate. A properly witnessed mark is considered a valid signature under law, so no special notarial certificate is required. For acknowledgments filed in California, Notaries must use the all-purpose form; jurats require the regular jurat wording.

Notarizing for Minors

Under Age 18. Generally, persons must reach the age of majority before they can handle their own legal affairs and sign documents for themselves. In California the age of majority is 18. Normally, parents or guardians will sign on a minor's behalf. In certain cases, where minors are engaged in business transactions or serving as court witnesses, they may lawfully sign documents and have their signatures notarized.

Include Age Next to Signature. When notarizing for a minor, the Notary should ask the young signer to write his or her age next to the signature to alert any person relying on the document that the signer is a minor. The Notary is not required to verify the minor signer's age.

Identification. The method for identifying a minor is the same as that for an adult. Because minors often do not possess acceptable identification documents, such as driver's licenses or passports, determining the identity of a minor can be a problem. If the minor does not have an acceptable ID, then the other methods of identifying acknowledgers must be used, either the Notary's personal knowledge of the minor or the oath of a credible identifying witness — or witnesses — who can identify the minor. (See "Credible Identifying Witness(es)," pages 42–44.)

Authentication

Documents Sent Out of State. Documents notarized in California and sent to other states may be required to bear proof that the Notary's signature and seal are genuine and that the Notary had authority to act at the time of notarization. This process of proving the genuineness of an official signature and seal is called *authentication* or *legalization*.

In California, the proof is in the form of an authenticating certificate attached to a notarized document by either the County Clerk's office where the Notary's oath and bond are filed or the office of the California Secretary of State. These certificates are also known as certificates of authority, certificates of capacity, certificates of authenticity, certificates of prothonotary and "flags"

The fee for an authenticating certificate from the County Clerk will vary from county to county. An authenticating certificate from the California Secretary of State costs $20 through the mail (check made out to "Secretary of State") and takes about two weeks to process. The original notarized document, a cover letter indicating the destination state or country and an addressed, postage-paid return envelope must be included. This should all be sent to:

> Office of Secretary of State
> Notary Public Section
> P.O. Box 942877
> Sacramento, CA 94277-0001

In person, an authenticating certificate from the California Secretary of State may be obtained at: 1500 11th Street, second floor, in Sacramento. For in-person pick up and processing while you wait, the cost is $26. An appointment is not necessary. It is not the Notary's responsibility to pick up or pay for the certificate of authority. Additional information is available by calling the Secretary of State's Notary Public Section at 1-916-653-3595.

Documents Sent Out of Country. If the notarized document is going out of the United States, a chain authentication process may be necessary, and additional certificates of authority may have to be obtained from the U.S. Department of State in Washington, D.C., a foreign consulate in Washington, D.C., and a ministry of foreign affairs in the particular foreign nation.

Apostilles and the Hague Convention. Over 60 nations, including the United States, subscribe to a treaty under auspices of the Hague Conference that simplifies authentication of notarized documents exchanged between these nations. The official name of this treaty, adopted by the Conference on October 5, 1961, is the "Hague Convention Abolishing the Requirement of Legalization for Foreign Public Documents." For a list of the subscribing countries, see "Hague Convention Nations," pages 113–115.

Under the Hague Convention, only one authenticating certificate called an *apostille* is necessary to ensure acceptance in these subscribing countries. (*Apostille* is French for "notation".)

In California, *apostilles* are issued by the Secretary of State's office. The procedure and fees are the same as for obtaining an ordinary authenticating certificate. Ensure that the country for which the document is destined is also specified.

Unauthorized Practice of Law

Do Not Assist in Legal Matters. A nonattorney Notary may not give legal advice or accept fees for legal advice. The nonattorney Notary may not assist a signer to draft, prepare, select, complete or understand a document or transaction. A Notary may only be responsible for the information on the notarial certificate.

Notaries may complete legal documents in which they are named as a subscribing party, but may never notarize their own signatures. Notaries involved in the unauthorized practice of law may have their commissions revoked and be criminally prosecuted. (Government Code, Section 8214.1 and Business and Professions Code, Section 6125)

Exceptions. Specially trained, nonattorney Notaries certified or licensed in a particular field (e.g., real estate) may offer advice in that field only. Paralegals under the supervision of an attorney may give advice about documents in routine legal matters.

Advertising

False or Misleading Advertising. A Notary's commission can be revoked or suspended if the Notary uses false or misleading advertising to misrepresent the authority, rights and privileges of a Notary. In addition, a fine of up to $1,500 may be imposed. (Government Code, Sections 8214.1 and 8214.15)

Foreign-Language Advertising. A nonattorney Notary advertising notarial services in a foreign language must take steps to guard against misinterpretation of his or her function as a Notary. Nonattorney Notaries are required to include in any such foreign-language advertisement the following in English and the foreign language: (Government Code, Section 8219.5)

1) The statement: "I am not an attorney and, therefore, cannot give legal advice about immigration or any other legal matters"; and

2) The fees a Notary is allowed to charge.

The above applies to signs and all other forms of written communication (e.g., business cards, telephone book ads) with the exception of a single desk plaque. Furthermore, literal translation of "Notary Public" into Spanish (*Notario Publico*) is prohibited by law. For violations, a Notary's commission can be suspended for a year or revoked — and on the second offense, it must be revoked permanently. (Government Code, Section 8219.5 and Business and Professions Code, Section 22442.3)

Immigration Expert. No person who claims to be an immigration expert or counselor may also advertise as a Notary Public. This provision attempts to counter self-styled immigration counselors from misrepresenting their authority. Violators may be fined up to $1,500. (Government Code, Section 8223)

Foreign Languages

Foreign-Language Documents. California Notaries are not expressly prohibited from notarizing a non-English document. However, the notarial certificate and document signature should be in English or in a language the Notary can read.

There are difficulties to consider with foreign-language documents: A blatant fraud might be undetectable; the U.S. Notary seal might be misinterpreted in another country; and making an informed journal entry might be difficult.

Foreign-Language Signers. There always should be direct communication between the Notary and document signer — whether in English or another language. The Notary should never rely on an intermediary or interpreter to determine a signer's willingness or competence. A third party may have reasons to misrepresent the transaction to the Notary and/or to the signer.

Immigration

Documents. Certain immigration documents may be notarized, such as the Affidavit of Support (I-134/I-864). However, state law does pose certain restrictions on the Notary in the area of immigration. Notaries should strictly adhere to these laws.

As of January 1, 1999, a nonattorney Notary also bonded as an immigration consultant may enter data provided by a client on state or federal immigration forms. Violators may be fined up to $750. (Government Code, Sections 8214.1, 8214.15 and 8223)

Advertising. No person who claims to be an immigration expert or counselor may also advertise as a Notary Public. This provision is designed to prevent self-styled immigration counselors from misrepresenting their powers to unsuspecting foreigners. Violators may have their Notary commissions revoked or suspended or be fined up to $1,500. (Government Code, Sections 8214.1, 8214.15 and 8223, and Business and Professions Code, Section 22442.3)

Identifying Signers. In notarizing forms that will be submitted to the U.S. Immigration and Naturalization Service (INS), and those forms *only*, a Notary may accept as proof of identity any ID or documentation acceptable to the INS, including a resident alien ID ("green card"). (Government Code, Section 8230)

Naturalization Certificates. A Notary may be in violation of federal law if he or she makes a typewritten, photostatic, or any other copy of a certificate of naturalization or notarizes it. (U.S. Penal Code, Section 75 and U.S. Code, Title 18, Section 137)

False Certificate. It can be a misdemeanor for a Notary to knowingly and for payment make a false notarial certificate on a document related to immigration. The Notary may be imprisoned in a county jail for a period not exceeding six months, be fined up to $2,500, or both. (Penal Code, Section 653.55)

Military-Base Notaries

Qualifications. The California Secretary of State may appoint Notaries for military bases of the U.S. Army, Navy, Coast Guard, Air Force, and Marine Corps in the state. These military-base Notaries must: (Government Code, Sections 8203.1 to 8203.3)

1) Be citizens of the United States;

2) Be not less than 18 years old;

3) Have successfully completed the Notary examination;

4) Be federal civil service employees at the base where they will act; and

5) Receive the recommendation of the base commanding officer.

Term of Office. The military-base Notary is commissioned for four years. However, this person ceases to be a Notary whenever he or she ceases to be employed as a civil service employee at the base where appointed. The commanding officer must notify the Secretary of State within 30 days of termination of the Notary's employment. (Government Code, Section 8203.4)

Jurisdiction. Military-base Notaries can notarize only at the base where they were appointed. (Government Code, Sections 8203.2)

Fees. Military-base Notaries may not charge for notarial services. (Government Code, Sections 8203.6)

Certificates. On notarial certificates, military-base Notaries must include the name of the base where the document was notarized. (Government Code, Sections 8203.5)

Military Officer Notarizations

May Notarize Worldwide. Certain U.S. military officers may notarize for military personnel and their dependents anywhere in the world. Under statutory authority, the following persons are authorized to act as Notaries:

- Civilian attorneys employed as legal assistance attorneys and licensed to practice law in the United States.

- Judge advocates on active duty or training as reservists on inactive duty.

- All adjutants, assistant adjutants, acting adjutants and personnel adjutants.

- Enlisted paralegals, personnel rank E-4 or higher, on active duty or training on inactive duty.

- Active duty personnel who are commissioned officers or senior noncommissioned officers (rank E-7 or higher) who are stationed at a Geographically Separated Unit (GSU) or location where no authorized Notary official is available, and who are appointed in writing by the unit's servicing general courtmartial convening authority.

Certificate. When signing documents in their official capacity, military-officer Notaries must specify the date and location of the notarization, their title and office, and use a raised seal or inked stamp citing Title 10 U.S.C. 1044a. (U.S. Code, Title 10, Sections 936, 1044a)

Authentication. Authentication of a military-officer notarization certificate is not required.

Wills

State Bar Advice. In the *California Notary Public Handbook* issued to all Notaries by the Notary Public Section of the Secretary of State's office, the following is printed:

> The California State Bar advises that when a Notary Public is asked to notarize a document which purports to be a will, the Notary Public should decline and advise the person requesting the notarization to consult a member of the California State Bar.

Special Circumstances. A Notary may notarize a will if the would-be testator (or *testatrix* for a woman) is following the advice of an attorney, but *only* if notarial wording is provided. The Notary cannot advise the signer on how to proceed. Wills probated in California generally do not require notarization, though they must be witnessed. However, a California Notary may be asked to notarize a will that will be probated in another state.

Do Not Offer Advice. A Notary risks prosecution for the unauthorized practice of law in advising a signer how to proceed with a will. Ill-informed advice may adversely affect the affairs of the signer. The format of a will is dictated by strict laws; any deviation may result in nullification. In some cases, holographic (handwritten) wills have been voided by notarization.

Living Wills. Documents popularly called "living wills" may be notarized. These are not actual wills, but written statements of a signer's wishes concerning medical treatment in the event he or she is unable to give instructions on his or her own behalf.

Durable Powers of Attorney for Health Care

Witness' Signature Required. A durable power of attorney for health care authorizes a person to make health care decisions for a principal if the principal is incapacitated. The instrument is considered legally valid if it contains the date of execution and is signed by the principal or in the principal's name by another person directed by that principal. (Probate Code, Section 4121)

The instrument may either be witnessed by two persons or acknowledged by the principal before a Notary. If witnessed by two people, the witnesses must be adults, must witness the signing or acknowledgment of the instrument and must sign a witness' statement as prescribed by Probate Code Section 4701. (Probate Code, Section 4701)

At least one witness shall be a person who is not related to the principal by blood, marriage or adoption and does not have an interest in the principal's estate. In addition, none of the following may act as a witness: (Probate Code, Sections 4122 and 4701)

- An attorney in fact of the principal;

- The principal's health care provider or an employee of that health care provider; or

- The operator or an employee of a community or residential care facility.

If a durable power of attorney is executed by a patient in a skilled nursing facility, a patient advocate or ombudsman must sign either as one of the two required witnesses or in addition to the notarization. The patient advocate or ombudsman shall make a declaration that he or she is serving as a witness in accordance with the provisions of Probate Code, Section 4701(e). A "skilled nursing facility" is defined in the California Health and Safety Code, Section 1250(a)(2)(c) as "a health facility that provides skilled nursing care and supportive care to patients whose primary need is for availability of skilled nursing care on an extended basis." (Probate Code, Section 4701)

Confidential Marriage Certificate

Restrictions. Only specially screened Notaries may issue and notarize confidential marriage certificates. To receive such authorization, a Notary must file an application along with a $175 annual fee with the County Clerk of the county in which the Notary resides.

After a background check and a two-hour course of instruction, the County Clerk may issue an authorization for the Notary to execute these certificates. This authorization requires annual renewal. (Family Code, Sections 530–536)

Certificates and Fees. Blank confidential marriage certificates are provided to authorized Notaries by the County Clerk for a fee, which the Notary may charge to the married couple along with the notarial fee for a jurat. (Family Code, Section 503)

Cannot Perform Marriages. Although a California Notary may

issue and notarize confidential marriage certificates, the Notary cannot perform the actual marriage ceremony unless he or she is also a member of the clergy or an official authorized to solemnize marriages.

Digital Signatures

Recognized by State. California law recognizes the existence of digital signatures. Public agencies are allowed — but *not* required — to accept and recognize digital signatures as having the same effect as a hand-made signature. (Government Code, Section 16.5)

A digital signature is an electronic identifier, created by computer that: (Government Code, Section 16.5)

1) Is unique to the person using it;

2) Is capable of verification;

3) Is under the sole control of the person using it; and

4) Is linked to data in such a manner that if the data is changed, the digital signature is invalidated.

No Notarization Procedures Established. Notaries should *not* attempt to notarize digital signatures as there are now no statutory procedures for doing so. In addition, the use of a digital or computer-affixed Notary seal is prohibited by law.

MISCONDUCT, FINES AND PENALTIES

Misconduct

Application Misstatement. Substantial and material misstatement or omission in the application for a Notary commission is reason for the Secretary of State to revoke, suspend or refuse to grant a Notary's commission. (Government Code, Section 8214.1)

Felony Conviction. Conviction for a felony or any offense involving moral depravity or of a nature incompatible with notarial duties, such as a forgery conviction, is reason for the Secretary of State to revoke, suspend or refuse to grant a Notary's commission. Pleading *nolo contendere* (no contest) is considered a conviction. (Government Code, Section 8214.1)

Professional Misconduct. Revocation, suspension, restriction, or denial of a professional license for misconduct, dishonesty, or any cause substantially relating to notarial duties or responsibilities is reason for the Secretary of State to revoke, suspend or refuse to grant a Notary's commission. (Government Code, Section 8214.1)

Failure of Duty. Failure to fully and faithfully discharge the duties or responsibilities of a Notary, such as in failing to keep a journal of notarial acts, is reason for the Secretary of State to refuse to grant or to revoke or suspend a Notary's commission. In addition, a fine of up to $750 may be imposed. (Government Code, Sections 8214.1 and 8214.15)

Falsely Acting as a Notary. Any person who is not a Notary and who represents himself or herself as a Notary in relation to any document affecting title to, or placing an encumbrance or interest secured by a mortgage or trust deed on, real property of certain single-family residences, is guilty of a felony. (Government Code, Section 8227.3)

Making False Statements to Notary. Any person who knowingly makes a false sworn statement to a Notary to induce the Notary to perform improper notarizations with regard to documents described above is guilty of a felony. (Penal Code, Section 115.5)

False or Misleading Advertising. The use of false or misleading advertising by a Notary to represent that he or she has duties, rights and privileges not given by law is reason for the Secretary of State to revoke, suspend or refuse to grant a Notary's commission. (Government Code, Sections 8214.1 and 8214.15)

Improper Foreign-Language Advertising. For failing to include in the advertisement, in English and the foreign language, the statement, "I am not an attorney and, therefore, cannot give legal advice about immigration or any other legal matters," or failing to include the fees a Notary is allowed to charge, or for including a literal Spanish translation of the words "Notary Public" (*Notario Publico* or *Notaria Publica*), a Notary's commission can be suspended for a year or revoked — and on the second offense revoked permanently. (Government Code, Section 8219.5)

Advertising as Immigration Expert. No person who claims to

be an immigration expert or counselor may also advertise as a Notary Public. This provision is designed to prevent self-styled immigration counselors from misrepresenting their powers to unsuspecting foreigners. Violation of the law relating to immigration matters and advertising is reason for the Secretary of State to revoke, suspend or refuse to grant a Notary's commission. (Government Code, Sections 8214.1 and 8223)

Unauthorized Practice of Law. The unauthorized practice of law — giving advice on legal matters when one is not a lawyer — is reason for the Secretary of State to deny, revoke or suspend a Notary's commission. (Government Code, Section 8214.1)

Overcharging. Charging more than the legally prescribed fees is reason for the Secretary of State State to revoke, suspend or refuse to grant a Notary's commission. In addition, a fine of up to $750 may be imposed. (Government Code, Sections 8214.1 and 8214.15)

Dishonesty or Fraud. Commission of an act involving dishonesty, fraud, or deceit with the intent to substantially benefit the Notary or another, or substantially injure another, is reason for the Secretary of State to revoke, suspend or refuse to grant a Notary's commission. In addition, a fine of up to $1,500 may be imposed. (Government Code, Sections 8214.1 and 8214.15)

Intent to Defraud — Real Property. Any Notary who knowingly and willfully performs a notarial act with intent to defraud in relation to a deed of trust on real property (no more than four dwelling units) with knowledge that the deed contains false information or is forged is guilty of a felony. (Government Code, Section 8214.2)

Recording False Instruments. Any person who knowingly records a false or forged document for real property as described above, in addition to other penalties, may be fined up to $75,000. (Penal Code, Section 115.5)

Found Liable for Fraud. Being found liable for damages in a suit accusing fraud, misrepresentation, or violation of state laws is reason for the Secretary of State to revoke, suspend or deny a Notary's commission. (Government Code, Section 8214.1)

Incomplete Acknowledgment. Failure to complete an acknowledgment at the same time the Notary's signature and seal are affixed to the document is reason for the Secretary of State to revoke, suspend or refuse to grant a Notary's commission. In addition, a fine of up to $750 may be imposed. (Government Code, Sections 8214.1 and 8214.15)

False Certificate. A Notary who knowingly completes a false notarial certificate is guilty of a misdemeanor and subject to criminal penalties. Further, the Notary may have his or her commission suspended or revoked and be fined up to $1,500. A Notary would be completing a false certificate, for example, if he or she signed and sealed an acknowledgment certificate indicating a signer personally appeared when the signer actually did not. (Government Code, Sections 6203, 8214.1 and 8214.15)

False Certificate on Immigration Document. It can be a misdemeanor for a Notary knowingly and for payment to make a false notarial certificate on a document related to immigration. The punishment may be imprisonment in the county jail for a period not exceeding six months, or a fine not exceeding $2,500, or both. (Penal Code, Section 653.55)

Naturalization Certificate Copies or Notarizations. A Notary may be in violation of federal law if he or she makes a typewritten, photostatic, or any other copy of a certificate of naturalization or notarizes it. (U.S. Penal Code, Section 75 and U.S.Code, Title 18, Section 137)

Oath or Affirmation Not Administered. Failure to administer any oath or affirmation as required by law is reason for the Secretary of State to revoke, suspend or refuse to grant a Notary's commission. In addition, a fine of up to $750 may be imposed. (Government Code, Sections 8214.1 and 8214.15)

Journal Not Delivered. If a Notary refuses to deliver notarial records to the County Clerk as specified by law, the Notary is guilty of a misdemeanor and is liable for damages suffered by any person as a result. (Government Code, Section 8209)

Failure to Secure Journal or Seal. A Notary's failure to keep the official journal and seal in a locked and secured area may result in revocation or suspension of the Notary's commission. (Government Code, Section 8214.1)

Misuse of Seal. Any person who, with intent to defraud, forges or counterfeits a Notary seal to give a document the appearance of being government-issued is guilty of forgery. Documents may include, but are not limited to, an identification card, driver's license, birth certificate, passport or Social Security card. In addition, forgery is punishable by imprisonment for up to one year. (Penal Code, Sections 472 and 473)

Use of Seal for Endorsement or Testimonial. Notaries may not use the official seal to endorse or promote any product, service or contest. The Notary seal may only be used to carry out the official duties of a Notary Public. (Government Code, Section 8207)

Lost or Damaged Seal. Failure to report that a seal is lost, misplaced, destroyed, broken, damaged or otherwise unworkable can result in a $1,500 fine. (Government Code, Sections 8207.3 and 8207.4)

Certificate of Authorization Procedure Violation. The failure of a Notary or vendor to comply with procedures regarding the Certificate of Authorization in purchasing or selling a Notary seal can result in a $1,500 fine for each violation. Such a penalty would result from a civil lawsuit initiated by the state attorney general or a local district attorney, city attorney or prosecutor. (Government Code, Sections 8207.2, 8207.3 and 8207.4)

Nonpayment of Judgment. Failure to submit any remittance to the Secretary of State or to satisfy any court-ordered money judgment, including restitution, is reason for the Secretary of State to revoke, suspend or refuse to grant a Notary commission. (Government Code, Section 8214.1)

Delinquency on Child Support Payments. The Secretary of State is prohibited from issuing or renewing a Notary commission for any person who has not complied with child support orders. Any commission fees that have been paid by the applicant will not be refunded. (Welfare and Institutions Code, Section 11350.6)

Cancellation of Commission. The Secretary of State may

cancel the commission of a Notary Public if any of the commission fees are not paid due to a returned check. Upon receiving notice from a financial institution that the check or draft was not honored, the Secretary of State will give written notice to the applicant requesting payment by cashier's check. Should the Secretary of State need to issue a second notice, the commission will be cancelled effective the date of that second notice. (Government Code, Section 8204.1)

Liability for Damages. A Notary and the surety company bonding the Notary may be sued by any person who has been damaged by the Notary's official acts. The surety is liable only up to the amount of the bond, but a Notary may be found liable for any amount of money. (Government Code, Section 8214)

Right to a Hearing

Revocation, Suspension or Denial. Before a commission can be revoked or suspended, or after a commission is denied, the Notary or applicant has the right to a hearing. However, after denial of a Notary commission, an applicant has no right to a hearing when, within one year prior to the application, the Secretary of State has duly found that the applicant has committed or omitted acts constituting grounds for suspension or revocation of a Notary commission. (Government Code, Section 8214.3)

Resignation Will Not Stop Investigation. If a Notary under investigation should resign or let his or her commission expire, the Secretary of State may still press the investigation and/or disciplinary proceedings. A record will then be made indicating whether the findings would have caused commission suspension or revocation. (Government Code, Section 8214.4)

Filed with County Clerk. When a Notary's commission is revoked, a copy of the revocation is filed by the Secretary of State with the County Clerk of the county where the Notary has filed an oath and bond. The County Clerk then notes the revocation and the revocation date in the clerk's official records. (Government Code, Section 8214.5) ■

Test Your Knowledge

Trial Exam

Instructions. This examination is designed to test your
knowledge of the basic concepts of notarization. It will also
help you prepare for the proctored California Notary Public
exam that you must pass before being commissioned as a
California Notary. The questions here, of course, are not the
same as those on the official test. Also, the Notary Public exam
is made up of 25 multiple-choice questions, with no true/false
or essay questions as in this trial exam.

Work through the exam without looking at the answers,
then check your responses and note where you need additional
study. Careful review of "Notary Laws Explained" (pages 18–72),
the reprinted Notary statutes (pages 79–103), "10 Most-Asked
Questions" (pages 9–13) and "Steps to Proper Notarization"
(pages 14–17) will produce the answers.

A perfect score on this examination is 100 points. There are:

- 20 true/false questions worth 1 point each
- 5 multiple-choice questions worth 4 points each
- 5 fill-in-the-blank questions worth 4 points each
- 5 essay questions worth 8 points each.

Now, get a separate sheet of paper and a pen or pencil, and
get ready to test your knowledge.

Part 1: True/False. For the following statements, answer true
or false. Each correct answer is worth 1 point:

1. Notaries may act only in the county where they are

commissioned. True or false?

2. The maximum Notary fee for taking the acknowledgment of three signers is $15. True or false?

3. It is a Notary's duty to serve all persons requesting lawful notarial acts, even those who are not customers. True or false?

4. Notaries must keep a photocopy of every document notarized. True or false?

5. A deposition is oral testimony that is written down and used as evidence in a court proceeding. True or false?

6. Notaries can withhold their services if they believe a signer is unable to understand a document. True or false?

7. It is a Notary's duty to draft powers of attorney, mortgages, and deeds, upon request. True or false?

8. The letters "L.S." stand for the Latin words *locus sigilli*, which mean "location of the seal." True or false?

9. Holographic wills must be notarized to be valid. True or false?

10. A Notary may rely on two strangers as credible identifying witnesses as long as both witnesses have good photo IDs. True or false?

11. A Notary can notarize documents which he or she will be signing as a corporate officer. True or false?

12. A signer of a homestead agreement for property in California must leave a right thumbprint in the Notary's journal. True or false?

13. The Notary needn't reimburse the surety company for bond funds paid out to a person financially harmed by the Notary's actions. True or false?

14. A Notary is not obligated to determine whether a signer does indeed have authority to sign as a corporate officer. True or false?

15. A Notary's seal and journal belong to the Notary's employer if the employer paid for them. True or false?

16. The all-purpose certificate is not to be used for jurats or proofs of execution by a subscribing witness. True or false?

17. An affirmation is the legal equivalent of an oath, but has no reference to a Supreme Being. True or false?

18. Extra recording fees are imposed on loose Notary certificates that are not exactly 8½ by 11 inches in size. True or false?

19. Notaries may not refuse to notarize blank or incomplete documents if they are signed in the Notary's presence. True or false?

20. A nonattorney Notary may not charge more than $10 for secretarial services related to a person's immigration application. True or false?

Multiple Choice. Choose the one best answer to each question. Each correct answer is worth 4 points.

1. A Notary has a disqualifying interest when acting as...
    a. An attorney who has drafted papers for a client.
    b. A real estate agent selling a condominium.
    c. A mortgagor in a real estate transaction.

2. To become a Notary, an applicant must...
    a. Have been a state resident for at least one year.
    b. Be fingerprinted and report all previous names.
    c. Pass an oral exam given by the Governor's office.

3. A certificate of authority for a Notary may be obtained...
    a. From the Governor's office or the County Clerk.
    b. From a stationery store or the Notary himself/herself.
    c. From the Secretary of State or the County Clerk.

4. "Satisfactory evidence" of identity means reliance on...
    a. ID cards or (a) credible identifying witness(es).
    b. ID cards or personal knowledge of identity.
    c. A credible identifying witness or personal knowledge.

5. A California Notary may...
    a. Take depositions and affidavits.
    b. Advertise that he or she is an immigration consultant.
    c. Certify a copy of a foreign birth certificate.

<u>Fill in the Blank</u>. Write in the word or phrase that best completes each sentence. Each correct answer is worth 4 points.

1. The Notary and the Notary's _____ are liable for the Notary's neglect or official misconduct.

2. A solemn, spoken pledge that is not an affirmation is called an _____.

3. An acceptable ID card should contain a signature, a description and a _____ of its bearer.

4. A certified copy certifies the _____ of the reproduction.

5. Wills written entirely in the testator's own handwriting are called _____.

<u>Essay</u>. Reply to each question or statement with a short paragraph. Each complete and correct response is worth 8 points.

1. Discuss the distinctions between a Notary bond and Notary errors and omissions insurance.

2. How does a proof of execution by subscribing witness work?

3. What is an *apostille* and when is it used?

4. Why should a Notary always complete the journal entry before filling out a notarial certificate?

5. Outline the differences between an acknowledgment certificate and a jurat.

Test Answers

<u>True/False</u>. 1. F; 2. F; 3. T; 4. F; 5. T; 6. T; 7. F; 8. T; 9. F; 10. T; 11. F; 12. F; 13. F; 14. T; 15. F; 16. T; 17. T; 18. T; 19. F; 20. T

<u>Multiple Choice</u>. 1. c; 2. b; 3. c; 4. a; 5. a

<u>Fill In The Blank</u>. 1. Surety; 2. Oath; 3. Photograph; 4. Accuracy; 5. Holographic

<u>Essay</u>. Responses should include the basic information in the paragraphs below:

1. A Notary bond, obtained through a state-licensed surety company, provides protection for the public in case of the Notary's negligence or intentional misconduct. Up to the cash limit of the bond, the surety agrees to pay damages to anyone who suffers a loss because of the Notary's actions; the Notary, however, then must reimburse the surety. Notary errors and omissions insurance, also purchased from a state-licensed company, protects the Notary in case of an unintentional error, up to the policy limit. The Notary does not reimburse the insurance company. A bond is required by law; errors and omissions insurance is not.

2. A proof of execution in lieu of an acknowledgment is sometimes resorted to when a document's principal signer is unavailable to appear before a Notary. In most such cases, the principal will be out of town, out of state or even out of the country. A so-called subscribing witness who has either seen the principal sign the document or taken the principal's acknowledgment of the signature may present this document to a Notary on the principal's behalf. The witness must sign ("subscribe") the document in addition to the principal. The witness, who must be personally known to the Notary, is given an oath by the Notary. A person who is a grantee or beneficiary of a document should not serve as a subscribing witness. In California, proofs of execution by subscribing witness may not be used with grant deeds, deeds of trust, quitclaim deeds, mortgages and security agreements.

3. An *apostille* is a certificate authenticating the signature and seal of a Notary that is issued under provisions of an

international treaty, signed by more than 60 nations, called the Hague Convention Abolishing the Requirement of Legalization for Foreign Public Documents. For notarized documents exchanged between the subscribing nations, this treaty streamlines the time-consuming authentication process known as "chain certification" by requiring only one authenticating certificate, the *apostille* (French for "notation"). *Apostilles* for California Notaries are issued by the Secretary of State.

4. Filling out a journal entry before completing a notarial certificate prevents a signer from taking the document and leaving before an important record of the notarization is made in the journal.

5. An acknowledgment certificate certifies that the signer of the document personally appeared before the Notary on the date and in the county indicated. It also certifies that the signer's identity was satisfactorily proven to the Notary and that the signer acknowledged having signed freely. A jurat certifies that the person signing the document did so in the Notary's presence, that the person appeared before the Notary on the date and in the county indicated, and that the Notary administered an oath or affirmation to the signer. Though it may not be required by law, the prudent Notary will always identify the signer in executing a jurat.

Tally Your Score

After checking your answers, add up your score. Then look at the grading scale below to determine how you stand:

- 90–100: Excellent!
- 80–89: Good, but some review needed.
- 70–79: Fair. Reread the parts of the *Primer* covering the answers you missed.
- Below 70: Below par. Study the laws thoroughly again. ■

California Laws Pertaining to Notaries Public

Reprinted on the following pages are pertinent sections of California statutes affecting Notaries and notarial acts, mostly drawn from the California Government Code and Civil Code. These statutes embody legislation in effect January 1, 1999.

CALIFORNIA STATUTES

GOVERNMENT CODE

§ 16.5. (a) In any written communication with a public entity, as defined in Section 811.2, in which a signature is required or used, any party to the communication may affix a signature by use of a digital signature that complies with the requirements of this section. The use of a digital signature shall have the same force and effect as the use of a manual signature if and only if it embodies all of the following attributes:

(1) It is unique to the person using it.

(2) It is capable of verification.

(3) It is under the sole control of the person using it.

(4) It is linked to data in such a manner that if the data are changed, the digital signature is invalidated.

(5) It conforms to regulations adopted by the Secretary of State. Initial regulations shall be adopted no later than January 1, 1997. In developing these regulations, the secretary shall seek the advice of public and private entities, including, but not limited to, the Department of Information Technology, the California Environmental Protection Agency, and the Department of General Services. Before the secretary adopts the regulations, he or she shall hold at least one public hearing to receive comments.

(b) The use or acceptance of a digital signature shall be at the option of the parties. Nothing in this section shall require a public entity to use or permit the use of a digital signature.

(c) Digital signatures employed pursuant to Section 71066 of the Public Resources Code are exempted from this section.

(d) "Digital signature" means an electronic identifier, created by computer, intended by the party using it to have the same force and effect as the use of a manual signature.

§ 1360. Unless otherwise provided, before any officer enters on the duties of his office, he shall take and subscribe the oath or affirmation set forth in Section 3 of Article XX of the Constitution of California.

§ 1362. Unless otherwise provided, the oath may be taken before any officer authorized to administer oaths.

§ 6100. Officers of the state, or of a county or judicial district, shall not perform any official services unless upon the payment of the fees prescribed by law for the performance of the services, except as provided in this chapter.

This section shall not be construed to prohibit any notary public, except a notary public whose fees are required by law to be remitted to the state or any other public agency, from performing notarial services without charging a fee.

§ 6107. (a) No public entity, including the state, a county, city, or other political subdivision, nor any officer or employee thereof, including notaries public, shall demand or receive any fee or compensation for doing any of the following:

(1) Recording, indexing, or issuing certified copies of any discharge, certificate of service, certificate of satisfactory service, notice of separation, or report of separation of any member of the armed forces of the United States.

(2) Furnishing a certified copy of, or searching for, any public record which is to be used in an application or claim for a pension, allotment, allowance, compensation, insurance (including automatic insurance), or any other benefits under any act of Congress for service in the armed forces of the United States or under any law of this state relating to veterans' benefits.

(3) Furnishing a certified copy of, or searching for, any public record which is required by the Veterans Administration to be used in determining the eligibility of any person to participate in benefits made available by the Veterans Administration.

(4) Rendering any other service in connection with an application or claim referred to in paragraph (2) or (3).

(b) The services referred to in subdivision (a) shall be rendered on request of a United States official, the claimant or applicant, or the guardian, conservator, or attorney of the claimant or applicant, or any other person acting on behalf of the claimant or applicant. A public officer or employee is liable on his or her official bond for failure or refusal to render the services.

§ 6108. No officer of a county or judicial district shall charge or receive any fee or compensation for administering or certifying the oath of office or for filing or swearing to any claim or demand against any county in the State.

§ 6109. Every officer of a county or judicial district, upon receiving any fees for official duty or service, may be required by the person paying the fees to make out in writing and to deliver to the person a particular account of the fees. The account shall specify for what the fees, respectively, accrued, and the officer shall receipt it. If the officer refuses or neglects to do so when required, he is liable to the person paying the fees in treble the amount so paid.

§ 6110. Upon payment of the fees required by law, the officer shall perform the services required. For every failure or refusal to do so, the officer is liable upon his official bond.

§ 6203. Every officer authorized by law to make or give any certificate or other writing is guilty of a misdemeanor if he makes and delivers as true any certificate or writing containing statements which he knows to be false.

§ 8200. The Secretary of State may appoint and commission notaries public in such number as the Secretary of State deems necessary for the public convenience. Notaries public may act as such notaries in any part of this state.

§ 8201. Every person appointed as notary public shall:

(a) Be at the time of appointment a legal resident of this state, except as otherwise provided in Section 8203.1.

(b) Be not less than 18 years of age.

(c) Have satisfactorily completed a written examination prescribed by the Secretary of State to determine the fitness of the person to exercise the functions of the office of notary public. All questions shall be based on the law of this state as set forth in the booklet of the laws of California relating to notaries public distributed by the Secretary of State.

§ 8201.1. Prior to granting an appointment as a notary public, the Secretary of State shall determine that the applicant possesses the required honesty, credibility, truthfulness, and integrity to fulfill the responsibilities of the position. To assist in determining the identity of the applicant and whether the applicant has been convicted of a disqualifying crime specified in subdivision (b) of Section 8214.1, the Secretary of State shall require that applicants be fingerprinted.

§ 8201.5. The Secretary of State shall require an applicant for appointment and commission as a notary public to complete an application form prescribed by the Secretary of State. Information on this form filed by an applicant with the Secretary of State, except for his name and address, is confidential and no individual record shall be divulged by an official or employee having access to it to any person other than the applicant, his authorized representative, or an employee or officer of the federal government, the state government, or a local agency, as defined in subdivision

(b) of Section 6252 of the Government Code, acting in his official capacity. Such information shall be used by the Secretary of State for the sole purpose of carrying out the duties of this chapter.

§ 8202.5. The Secretary of State may appoint and commission the number of state, city, county, and public school district employees as notaries public to act for and on behalf of the governmental entity for which appointed which the Secretary of State deems proper. Whenever a notary is appointed and commissioned, a duly authorized representative of the employing governmental entity shall execute a certificate that the appointment is made for the purposes of the employing governmental entity, and whenever the certificate is filed with any state or county officer, no fees shall be charged by the officer for the filing or issuance of any document in connection with the appointment. The state or any city, county, or school district for which the notary public is appointed and commissioned pursuant to this section may pay from any funds available for its support the premiums on any bond and the cost of any stamps, seals, or other supplies required in connection with the appointment, commission, or performance of the duties of the notary public.

Any fees collected or obtained by any notary public whose documents have been filed without charge and for whom bond premiums have been paid by the employer of the notary public shall be remitted by the notary public to the employing agency which shall deposit the funds to the credit of the fund from which the salary of the notary public is paid.

§ 8202.7. A private employer, pursuant to an agreement with an employee who is a notary public, may pay the premiums on any bond and the cost of any stamps, seals, or other supplies required in connection with the appointment, commission, or performance of the duties of such notary public. Such agreement may also provide for the remission of fees collected by such notary public to the employer, in which case any fees collected or obtained by such notary public while such agreement is in effect shall be remitted by such notary public to the employer which shall deposit such funds to the credit of the fund from which the compensation of the notary public is paid.

§ 8202.8. Notwithstanding any other provision of law, a private employer of a notary public who has entered into an agreement with his or her employee pursuant to Section 8202.7 may limit, during the employee's ordinary course of employment, the providing of notarial services by the employee solely to transactions directly associated with the business purposes of the employer.

§ 8203.1. The Secretary of State may appoint and commission notaries public for the military and naval reservations of the Army, Navy, Coast Guard, Air Force, and Marine Corps of the United States, wherever located in the state; provided, however, that such appointee shall be a citizen of the United States, not less than 18 years of age, and must meet the requirements set forth in subdivision (c) of Section 8201.

§ 8203.2. Such notaries public shall be appointed only upon the recommendation of the commanding officer of the reservation in which they are to act, and they shall be authorized to act only within the boundaries of this reservation.

§ 8203.3. In addition to the qualifications established in Section 8203.1, appointment will be made only from among those persons who are federal civil service employees at the reservation in which they will act as notaries public.

§ 8203.4. The term of office shall be as set forth in Section 8204, except that the appointment shall terminate if the person shall cease to be employed as a federal civil service employee at the reservation for which appointed. The commanding officer of the reservation shall notify the Secretary of State of termination of employment at the reservation for which appointed within 30 days of such termination. A notary public whose appointment terminates pursuant to this section will have such termination treated as a resignation.

§ 8203.5. In addition to the name of the State, the jurat shall also contain the name of the reservation in which the instrument is executed.

§ 8203.6. No fees shall be collected by such notaries public for service rendered within the reservation in the capacity of a notary public.

§ 8204. The term of office of a notary public is for four years commencing with the date specified in the commission.

§ 8204.1. The Secretary of State may cancel the commission of a notary public if a check or other remittance accepted as payment for the examination, application, commission, and fingerprint fee is not paid upon presentation to the financial institution upon which the check or other remittance was drawn. Upon receiving written notification that the item presented for payment has not been honored for payment, the Secretary of State shall first give a written notice of the applicability of this section to the notary public or the person submitting the instrument. Thereafter, if the amount is not paid by a cashier's check or the equivalent, the Secretary of State shall give a second written notice of cancellation and the cancellation shall thereupon be effective. This second notice shall be given at least 20 days after the first notice, and no more than 90 days after the commencement date of the commission.

§ 8205. (a) It is the duty of a notary public, when requested: (1) To demand acceptance and payment of foreign and inland bills of exchange, or promissory notes, to protest them for nonacceptance and nonpayment, and, with regard only to the nonacceptance or nonpayment of bills and notes, to exercise any other powers and duties that by the law of nations and according to commercial usages, or by the laws of any other state, government, or country, may be performed by notaries.

(2) To take the acknowledgment or proof of powers of attorney, mortgages, deeds, grants, transfers, and other instruments of writing executed by any person, and to give a certificate of that proof or acknowledgment, endorsed on or attached to the instrument. The certificate shall be signed by the notary public in the notary public' s own handwriting. A notary public may not accept any acknowledgment or proof of any instrument that is incomplete.

(3) To take depositions and affidavits, and administer oaths and affirmations, in all matters incident to the duties of the office, or to be used before any court, judge, officer, or board. Any deposition, affidavit, oath, or affirmation shall be signed by the notary public in the notary public's own handwriting.

(4) To certify copies of powers of attorney under Section 4307 of the Probate Code. The certification shall be signed by the notary public in the notary public's own handwriting.

(b) It shall further be the duty of a notary public, upon written request:

(1) To furnish to the Secretary of State certified copies of the notary's journal.

(2) To respond within 30 days of receiving written requests sent by certified mail from the Secretary of State's office for information relating to official acts performed by the notary.

§ 8206. (a) (1) A notary public shall keep one active sequential journal at a time, of all official acts performed as a notary public. The journal shall be kept in a locked and secured area, under the direct and exclusive control of the notary. Failure to secure the journal shall be cause for the Secretary of State to take administrative action against the commission held by the notary public pursuant to Section 8214.1.

(2) The journal shall be in addition to and apart from any copies of notarized documents that may be in the possession of the notary public and shall include all of the following:

(A) Date, time, and type of each official act.

(B) Character of every instrument acknowledged or proved before the notary.

(C) The signature of each person whose signature is being notarized.

(D) A statement as to whether the identity of a person making an acknowledgment was based on personal knowledge or satisfactory evidence. If identity was established by satisfactory evidence pursuant to Section 1185 of the Civil Code, then the journal shall contain the signature of the credible witness swearing or affirming to the identity of the individual or the type of identifying document, the governmental agency issuing the document, the serial or identifying number of the document, and the date of issue or expiration of the document.

(E) If the identity of the person making the acknowledgment was established by the oaths or affirmations of two credible witnesses whose identities are proven upon the presentation of satisfactory evidence, the type of identifying documents, the identifying numbers of the documents and the dates of issuance or expiration of the documents presented by the witnesses to establish their identity.

(F) The fee charged for the notarial service.

(G) If the document to be notarized is a deed, quitclaim deed, or deed of trust affecting real property, the notary public shall require the party signing the document to place his or her right thumbprint in the journal. If the right thumbprint is not available, then the notary shall have the party use his or her left thumb, or any available finger and shall so indicate in the journal. If the party signing the document is physically unable to provide a thumbprint or fingerprint, the notary shall so indicate in the journal and shall also provide an explanation of that physical condition. This paragraph shall not apply to a trustee's deed resulting from a decree of foreclosure or a nonjudicial foreclosure pursuant to Section 2924 of the Civil Code, nor to a deed of reconveyance.

(b) If a sequential journal of official acts performed by a notary public is stolen, lost, misplaced, destroyed, damaged, or otherwise rendered unusable as a record of notarial acts and information, the notary public shall immediately notify the Secretary of State by certified or registered mail. The notification shall include the period of the journal entries, the notary public commission number, and the expiration date of the commission, and when applicable, a photocopy of any police report that specifies the theft of the sequential journal of official acts.

(c) Upon written request of any member of the public, which request shall include the name of the parties, the type of document, and the month and year in which notarized, the notary shall supply a photostatic copy of the line item representing the requested transaction at a cost of not more than thirty cents ($0.30) per page.

(d) The journal of notarial acts of a notary public is the exclusive property of that notary public, and shall not be surrendered to an employer upon termination of employment, whether or not the employer paid for the journal, or at any other time. The notary public shall not surrender the journal to any other person, except the county clerk, pursuant to Section 8209, or to a peace officer, as defined in Sections 830.1, 830.2, and 830.3 of the Penal Code, acting in his or her official capacity and within his or her authority, in response to a criminal search warrant signed by a magistrate and served upon the notary public by the peace officer. The notary public shall obtain a receipt for the journal, and shall notify the Secretary of State by certified mail within 10 days that the journal was relinquished to a peace officer. The notification shall include the period of the journal entries, the commission number of the notary public, the expiration date of the commission, and a photocopy of the receipt. The notary public shall obtain a new sequential journal. If the journal relinquished to a peace officer is returned to the notary public and a new journal has been obtained, the notary public shall make no new entries in the returned journal. A notary public who is an employee shall permit inspection and copying of journal transactions by a duly designated auditor or agent of the notary public's employer, provided that the inspection and copying is done in the presence of the notary public and the transactions are directly associated with the business purposes of the employer. The notary public, upon the request of the employer, shall regularly provide copies of all transactions that are directly associated with the business purposes of the employer, but shall not be required to provide copies of any transaction that is unrelated to the employer's business. Confidentiality and safekeeping of any copies of the journal provided to the employer shall be the responsibility of that employer.

(e) The notary public shall provide the journal for examination and copying in the presence of the notary public upon receipt of a subpoena duces tecum or a court order, and shall certify those copies if requested.

§ 8207. A notary public shall provide and keep an official seal, which shall clearly show, when embossed, stamped, impressed or affixed to a document, the name of the notary, the State Seal, the words "Notary Public," and the name of the county wherein the bond and oath of office are filed, and the date the notary public's commission expires. The seal of every notary public commissioned on or after January 1, 1992, shall contain the sequential identification number assigned to the notary and the sequential identification number assigned to the manufacturer or vendor. The notary public shall authenticate with the official seal all official acts. A notary public shall not use the official notarial seal except for the purpose of carrying out the duties and responsibilities as set forth in this chapter. A notary public shall not use the title "notary public" except for the purpose of rendering notarial service.

The seal of every notary public shall be affixed by a seal press or stamp that will print or emboss a seal which legibly reproduces under photographic methods the required elements of the seal. The seal may be circular not over two inches in diameter, or may be a rectangular form of not more than one inch in width by two and one-half inches in length, with a serrated or milled edged border, and shall contain the information required by this section. The seal shall be kept in a locked and secured area, under the direct and exclusive control of the notary. Failure to secure the seal shall be cause for the Secretary of State to take administrative action against the commission held by the notary public pursuant to Section 8214.1.

The official seal of a notary public is the exclusive property of that notary public, and shall not be surrendered to an employer upon the termination of employment, whether or not the employer paid for the seal, or to any other person. The notary, or his or her representative, shall destroy or deface the seal upon termination, resignation, or revocation of the notary's commission.

This section shall become operative on January 1, 1992.

§ 8207.1. The Secretary of State shall assign a sequential identification number to each notary which shall appear on the notary commission.

This section shall become operative on January 1, 1992.

§ 8207.2. (a) No notary seal or press stamp shall be manufactured, duplicated, sold, or offered for sale unless authorized by the Secretary of State.

(b) The Secretary of State shall develop and implement procedures and guidelines for the issuance of notary seals on or before January 1, 1992.

(c) The Secretary of State shall issue a permit with a sequential identification number to each manufacturer or vendor authorized to issue notary seals. The Secretary of State may establish a fee for the issuance of the permit which shall not exceed the actual costs of issuing the permit.

(d) The Secretary of State shall develop a certificate of authorization to purchase a notary stamp from an authorized vendor.

(e) The certificate of authorization shall be designed to prevent forgeries and shall contain a sequential identification number.

(f) This section shall become operative on January 1, 1992.

§ 8207.3. (a) The Secretary of State shall issue certificates of authorization with which a notary public can obtain an official notary seal.

(b) A vendor or manufacturer is authorized to provide a notary with an official seal only upon presentation by the notary public of a certificate of authorization.

(c) A vendor of official seals shall note the receipt of certificates of authorization and sequential identification numbers of certificates presented by a notary public upon a certificate of authorization.

(d) A copy of a certificate of authorization shall be retained by a vendor and the original, which shall contain a sample impression of the seal issued to the notary public, shall be submitted to the Secretary of State for verification and recordkeeping. The Secretary of State shall develop guidelines for submitting certificates of authorization by vendors.

(e) Any notary whose official seal is lost, misplaced, destroyed, broken, damaged, or is rendered otherwise unworkable shall immediately mail or deliver written notice of that fact to the Secretary of State. The Secretary of State, within five working days after receipt of the notice, if requested by a notary, shall issue a certificate of authorization which a notary may use to obtain a replacement seal.

(f) This section shall become operative on January 1, 1992.

§ 8207.4. (a) Any person who willfully violates any part of Section 8207.1, 8207.2, 8207.3, or 8207.4 shall be subject to a civil penalty not to exceed one thousand five hundred dollars ($1,500) for each violation, which may be recovered in a civil action brought by the Attorney General or the district attorney or city attorney, or by a city prosecutor in any city and county.

(b) The penalty provided by this section is not an exclusive remedy, and does not affect any other relief or remedy provided by law.

(c) This section shall become operative on January 1, 1992.

§ 8208. The protest of a notary public, under his or her hand and official seal, of a bill of exchange or promissory note for nonacceptance or nonpayment, specifying any of the following is prima facie evidence of the facts recited therein:

(a) The time and place of presentment.

(b) The fact that presentment was made and the manner thereof.

(c) The cause or reason for protesting the bill.

(d) The demand made and the answer given, if any, or the fact that the drawee or acceptor could not be found.

§ 8209. (a) If any notary public resigns, is disqualified, removed from office, or allows his or her appointment to expire without obtaining reappointment within 30 days, all notarial records and papers shall be delivered within 30 days to the clerk of the county in which the notary public's current official oath of office is on file. If the notary public willfully fails or refuses to deliver all notarial records and papers to the county clerk within 30 days, the person is guilty of a misdemeanor and shall be personally liable for damages to any person injured by that action or inaction.

(b) In the case of the death of a notary public, the personal representative of the deceased shall promptly notify the Secretary of State of the death of the notary public and shall deliver all notarial records and papers of the deceased to the clerk of the county in which the notary public's official oath of office is on file.

(c) After 10 years from the date of deposit with the county clerk, if no request for, or reference to such records has been made, they may be destroyed upon order of court.

§ 8211. Fees charged by a notary public for the following services shall not exceed the fees prescribed by this section.

(a) For taking an acknowledgment or proof of a deed, or other instrument, to include the seal and the writing of the certificate, the sum of ten dollars ($10) for each signature taken.

(b) For administering an oath or affirmation to one person and executing the jurat, including the seal, the sum of ten dollars ($10).

(c) For all services rendered in connection with the taking of any deposition, the sum of twenty dollars ($20), and in addition thereto, the sum of five dollars ($5) for administering the oath to the witness and the sum of five dollars ($5) for the certificate to the deposition.

(d) For every protest for the nonpayment of a promissory note or for the nonpayment or nonacceptance of a bill of exchange, draft, or check, the sum of ten dollars ($10).

(e) For serving every notice of nonpayment of a promissory note or of nonpayment or nonacceptance of a bill of exchange, order, draft, or check, the sum of five dollars ($5).

(f) For recording every protest, the sum of five dollars ($5).

(g) No fee shall be charged to notarize signatures on absentee ballot identification envelopes or other voting materials.

(h) For certifying a copy of a power of attorney under Section 4307 of the Probate Code the sum of ten dollars ($10).

§ 8212. Every person appointed a notary public shall execute an official bond in the sum of fifteen thousand dollars ($15,000). The bond shall be in the form of a bond executed by an admitted surety insurer and not a deposit in lieu of bond.

§ 8213. (a) No later than 30 days after the beginning of the term prescribed in the commission, every person appointed a notary public shall file an official bond and an oath of office in the office of the county clerk of the county within which the person maintains a principal place of business as shown in the application submitted to the Secretary of State, and the commission shall not take effect unless this is done within the 30-day period. A person appointed to be a notary public shall take and subscribe the oath of office either in the office of that county clerk or before another notary public in that county. If the oath of office is taken and subscribed before a notary public, the oath and bond may be filed with the county clerk by certified mail. Upon the filing of the oath and bond, the county clerk shall immediately transmit to the Secretary of State a certificate setting forth the fact of the filing and containing a copy of the official oath, personally signed by the notary public in the form set forth in the commission and shall immediately deliver the bond to the county recorder for recording. The county clerk shall retain the oath of office for one year following the expiration of the term of the commission for which the oath was taken, after which the oath may be destroyed or otherwise disposed of. The copy of the oath, personally signed by the notary public, on file with the Secretary of State may at any time be read in evidence with like effect as the original oath, without further proof.

(b) If a notary public transfers the principal place of business from one county to another, the notary public may file a new oath of office and bond, or a duplicate of the original bond with the county clerk to which the principal place of business was transferred. If the notary public elects to make a new filing, the notary public shall, within 30 days of the filing, obtain an official seal which shall include the name of the county to which the notary public has transferred. In a case where the notary public elects to make a new filing, the same filing and recording fees are applicable as in the case of the original filing and recording of the bond.

(c) If a notary public submits an application for a name change to the Secretary of State, the notary public shall, within 30 days from the date an amended commission is issued, file a new oath of office and an amendment to the bond with the county clerk in which the principal place of business is located. The amended commission with the name change shall not take effect unless the filing is completed within the 30-day period. The amended commission with the name change takes effect the date the oath and amendment to the bond is filed with the county clerk. If the principal place of business address was changed in the application for name change, either a new or duplicate of the original bond shall be filed with the county clerk with the amendment to the bond. The notary public shall, within 30 days of the filing, obtain an official seal that includes the name of the notary public and the name of the county to which the notary public has transferred, if applicable.

(d) The recording fee specified in Section 27361 of the Government Code shall be paid by the person appointed a notary public. The fee may be paid to the county clerk who shall transmit it to the county recorder.

(e) The county recorder shall record the bond and shall thereafter mail, unless specified to the contrary, it to the person named in the instrument and, if no person is named, to the party leaving it for recording.

§ 8213.5. A notary public shall notify the Secretary of State by certified mail within 30 days as to any change in the location or address of the principal place of business or residence.

§ 8213.6. If a notary public changes his or her name, the notary public shall complete an application for name change form and file that application with the Secretary of State. Information on this form shall be subject to the confidentiality provisions described in Section 8201.5. Upon approval of the name change form, the Secretary of State shall issue a commission that reflects the new name of the notary public. The term of the commission and commission number shall remain the same.

§ 8214. For the official misconduct or neglect of a notary public, the notary public and the sureties on the notary public's official bond are liable in a civil action to the persons injured thereby for all the damages sustained.

§ 8214.1. The Secretary of State may refuse to appoint any person as notary public or may revoke or suspend the commission of any notary public upon any of the following grounds:

(a) Substantial and material misstatement or omission in the application submitted to the Secretary of State.

(b) Conviction of a felony, a lesser offense involving moral turpitude, or a lesser offense of a nature incompatible with the duties of a notary public. A conviction after a plea of nolo contendere is deemed to be a conviction within the meaning of this subdivision.

(c) Revocation, suspension, restriction, or denial of a professional license, if the revocation, suspension, restriction, or denial was for misconduct for dishonesty, or for any cause substantially relating to the duties or responsibilities of a notary public.

(d) Failure to discharge fully and faithfully any of the duties or responsibilities required of a notary public.

(e) When adjudged liable for damages in any suit grounded in fraud, misrepresentation, or violation of the state regulatory laws or in any suit based upon a failure to discharge fully and faithfully the duties as a notary public.

(f) The use of false or misleading advertising wherein the notary public has represented that the notary public has duties, rights, or privileges that he or she does not possess by law.

(g) The practice of law in violation of Section 6125 of the Business and Professions Code.

(h) Charging more than the fees prescribed by this chapter.

(i) Commission of any act involving dishonesty, fraud, or deceit with the intent to substantially benefit the notary public or another, or substantially injure another.

(j) Failure to complete the acknowledgment at the time the notary' s signature and seal are affixed to the document.

(k) Failure to administer the oath or affirmation as required by paragraph (3) of subdivision (a) of Section 8205.

(l) Execution of any certificate as a notary public containing a statement known to the notary public to be false.

(m) Violation of Section 8223.

(n) Failure to submit any remittance payable upon demand by the Secretary of State under this chapter or failure to satisfy any court-ordered money judgment, including restitution.

(o) Failure to secure the sequential journal of official acts, pursuant to Section 8206, or the official seal, pursuant to Section 8207.

(p) Violation of Section 8219.5.

§ 8214.15. (a) In addition to any commissioning or disciplinary sanction, a violation of subdivision (f), (i), (l), (m), or (p) of Section 8214.1, or a willful violation of subdivision (d) of Section 8214.1, is punishable by a civil penalty not to exceed one thousand five hundred dollars ($1,500).

(b) In addition to any commissioning or disciplinary sanction, a violation of subdivision (h), (j), or (k) of Section 8214.1, or a negligent violation of subdivision (d) of Section 8214.1, is punishable by a civil penalty not to exceed seven hundred fifty dollars ($750).

(c) The civil penalty may be imposed by the Secretary of State if a hearing is not requested pursuant to Section 8214.3. If a hearing is requested, the hearing officer shall make the determination.

(d) Any civil penalties collected pursuant to this section shall be transferred to the General Fund. It is the intent of the Legislature that to the extent General Fund moneys are raised by penalties collected pursuant to this section, that money should be made available to the Secretary of State's office to defray its costs of investigating and pursuing commissioning and monetary remedies for violations of the notary public law.

§ 8214.2. A notary public who knowingly and willfully with intent to defraud performs any notarial act in relation to a deed of trust on real property consisting of a single-family residence containing not more than four dwelling units, with knowledge that the deed of trust contains any false statements or is forged in whole or in part, is guilty of a felony.

§ 8214.3. Prior to a revocation or suspension pursuant to this chapter or after a denial of a commission, or prior to the imposition of a civil penalty, the person affected shall have a right to a hearing on the matter and the proceeding shall be conducted in accordance with Chapter 5 (commencing with Section 11500) of Part 1 of Division 3, except that a person shall not have a right to a hearing after a denial of an application for a notary public commission in either of the following cases:

(a) The Secretary of State has, within one year previous to the application, and after proceedings conducted in accordance with Chapter 5 (commencing with Section 11500) of Part 1 of Division 3, denied or revoked the applicant's application or commission.

(b) The Secretary of State has entered an order pursuant to Section 8214.4 finding that the applicant has committed or omitted acts constituting grounds for suspension or revocation of a notary public's commission.

§ 8214.4. Notwithstanding this chapter or Chapter 5 (commencing with Section 11500) of Part 1 of Division 3, if the Secretary of State determines, after proceedings conducted in accordance with Chapter 5 (commencing with Section 11500) of Part 1 of Division 3, that any notary public has committed or omitted acts constituting grounds for suspension or revocation of a notary public's commission, the resignation or expiration of the notary public's commission shall not bar the Secretary of State from instituting or continuing an investigation or instituting disciplinary proceedings. Upon completion of the disciplinary proceedings, the Secretary of State shall enter an order finding the facts and stating the conclusion that the facts would or would not have constituted grounds for suspension or revocation of the commission if the commission had still been in effect.

§ 8214.5. Whenever the Secretary of State revokes the commission of any notary public, the Secretary of State shall file with the county clerk of the county in which the notary public's principal place of business is located a copy of the revocation. The county clerk shall note such revocation and its date upon the original record of such certificate.

§ 8216. When a surety of a notary desires to be released from responsibility on account of future acts, the release shall be pursuant to Article 11 (commencing with Section 996.110), and not by cancellation or withdrawal pursuant to Article 13 (commencing with Section 996.310), of Chapter 2 of Title 14 of Part 2 of the Code of Civil Procedure. For this purpose the surety shall make application to the superior court of the county in which the notary public's principal place of business is located and the copy of the application and notice of hearing shall be served on the Secretary of State as the beneficiary.

§ 8219.5. (a) Every notary public who is not an attorney who advertises the services of a notary public in a language other than English by signs or other means of written communication, with the exception of a single desk plaque, shall post with that advertisement a notice in English and in the other language which sets forth the following:

(1) This statement: I am not an attorney and, therefore, cannot give legal advice about immigration or any other legal matters.

(2) The fees set by statute which a notary public may charge.

(b) The notice required by subdivision (a) shall be printed and posted as prescribed by the Secretary of State.

(c) Literal translation of the phrase "notary public" into Spanish, hereby defined as "notario publico" or "notario," is prohibited. For purposes of this sub-division, "literal translation" of a word or phrase from one language to another means the translation of a word or phrase without regard to the true meaning of the word or phrase in the language which is being translated.

(d) The Secretary of State shall suspend for a period of not less than one year or revoke the commission of any notary public who fails to comply with subdivision (a) or (c). However, on the second offense the commission of such notary public shall be revoked permanently.

§ 8220. The Secretary of State may adopt rules and regulations to carry out the provisions of this chapter. The regulations shall be adopted in accordance with the Administrative Procedure Act, Chapter 4.5 (commencing with Section 11371) of Part 1 of Division 3 of this title.

§ 8221. If any person shall knowingly destroy, deface, or conceal any records or papers belonging to the office of a notary public, such person shall be guilty of a misdemeanor and be liable in a civil action for damages to any person injured as a result of such destruction, defacing, or concealment.

§ 8222. (a) Whenever it appears to the Secretary of State that any person has engaged or is about to engage in any acts or practices which constitute or will constitute a violation of any provision of this chapter or any rule or regulation prescribed under the authority thereof, the Secretary of State may apply for an injunction, and upon a proper showing, any court of competent jurisdiction has power to issue a permanent or temporary injunction or restraining order to enforce the provisions of this chapter, and any party to the action has the right to prosecute an appeal from the order or judgment of the court.

(b) The court may order a person subject to an injunction or restraining order provided for in this section to reimburse the Secretary of State for expenses incurred in the investigation related to the petition. The Secretary of State shall refund any amount received as reimbursement should the injunction or restraining order be dissolved by an appellate court.

§ 8223. (a) No notary public who holds himself or herself out as being an immigration specialist, immigration consultant or any other title or description reflecting an expertise in immigration matters shall advertise in any manner whatsoever that he or she is a notary public.

(b) A notary public may enter data, provided by the client, on immigration forms provided by a federal or state agency. The fee for this service shall not exceed ten dollars ($10) per individual for each set of forms. If notary services are performed in relation to the set of immigration forms, additional fees may be collected pursuant to Section 8211. This fee limitation shall not apply to an attorney, who is also a notary public, who is rendering professional services regarding immigration matters.

(c) Nothing in this section shall be construed to exempt a notary public who enters data on an immigration form at the direction of a client, or otherwise performs the services of an immigration consultant, as defined by Section 22441 of the Business and Professions Code, from the requirements of Sections 22440 to 22447, inclusive, of the Business and Professions Code.

§ 8224. A notary public who has a direct financial or beneficial interest in a transaction shall not perform any notarial act in connection with such transaction.

For purposes of this section, a notary public has a direct financial or beneficial interest in a transaction if the notary public:

(a) With respect to a financial transaction, is named, individually, as a principal to the transaction.

(b) With respect to real property, is named, individually, as a grantor, grantee, mortgagor, mortgagee, trustor, trustee, beneficiary, vendor, vendee, lessor, or lessee, to the transaction.

For purposes of this section, a notary public has no direct financial or beneficial interest in a transaction where the notary public acts in the capacity of an agent, employee, insurer, attorney, escrow, or lender for a person having a direct financial or beneficial interest in the transaction.

§ 8224.1. A notary public shall not take the acknowledgment or proof of instruments of writing executed by the notary public nor shall depositions or affidavits of the notary public be taken by the notary public.

§ 8225. Any person who solicits, coerces, or in any manner influences a notary public to perform an improper notarial act knowing such act to be an improper notarial act shall be guilty of a misdemeanor.

§ 8227.1. It shall be a misdemeanor for any person who is not a duly commissioned, qualified, and acting notary public for the State of California to do any of the following:

(a) Represent or hold himself or herself out to the public or to any person as being entitled to act as a notary public.

(b) Assume, use or advertise the title of notary public in such a manner as to convey the impression that the person is a notary public.

(c) Purport to act as a notary public.

§ 8227.3. Any person who is not a duly commissioned, qualified, and acting notary public who does any of the acts prohibited by Section 8227.1 in relation to any document or instrument affecting title to, placing an encumbrance on, or placing an interest secured by a mortgage or deed of trust on, real property consisting of a single-family residence containing not more than four dwelling units, is guilty of a felony.

§ 8228. The Secretary of State may enforce the provisions of this chapter through the examination of a notary public's books, records, letters, contracts, and other pertinent documents relating to the official acts of the notary public.

§ 8230. If a notary public executes a jurat and the statement sworn or subscribed to is contained in a document purporting to identify the affiant, and includes the birthdate or age of the person and a purported photograph or finger or thumbprint of the person so swearing or subscribing, the notary public shall require, as a condition to executing the jurat, that the person verify the birthdate or age contained in the statement by showing either:

(a) A certified copy of the person's birth certificate, or

(b) An identification card or driver's license issued by the Department of Motor Vehicles.

For the purposes of preparing for submission of forms required by the United States Immigration and Naturalization Service, and only for such purposes, a notary public may also accept for identification any documents or declarations acceptable to the United States Immigration and Naturalization Service.

§ 27287. Unless it belongs to the class provided for in either Sections 27282 to 27286, inclusive, or Sections 1202 or 1203, of the Civil Code, or is a fictitious mortgage or deed of trust as provided in Sections 2952, or 2963, of the Civil Code, or is a fictitious oil and gas lease as provided in Section 1219 of the Civil Code, or is a claim of lien, as provided in Section 3084 of the Civil Code, or a notice of completion, as provided in Section 3093 of the Civil Code, before an instrument can be recorded its execution shall be acknowledged by the person executing it, or if executed by a corporation, by its president or secretary or other person executing it on behalf of the corporation, or, except for any grant deed other than a trustee's deed or a deed of reconveyance, mortgage, deed of trust, or security agreement, proved by subscribing witness or as provided in Sections 1198 and 1199 of the Civil Code, and the acknowledgment or proof certified as prescribed by law.

§ 27361. (a) The fee for recording and indexing every instrument, paper, or notice required or permitted by law to be recorded is four dollars ($4) for recording the first page and three dollars ($3) for each additional page, except the recorder may charge additional fees as follows:

(1) If the printing on printed forms is spaced more than nine lines per vertical inch or more than 22 characters and spaces per inch measured horizontally for not less than 3 inches in one sentence, the recorder shall charge one dollar ($1) extra for each page or sheet on which printing appears excepting, however, the extra charge shall not apply to printed words which are directive or explanatory in nature for completion of the form or on vital statistics forms. Fees collected under this paragraph are not subject to subdivision (b) or (c).

(2) If a page or sheet does not conform with the dimensions described in subdivision (a) of Section 27361.5, the recorder shall charge three dollars ($3) extra per page or sheet of the document. The extra charge authorized under this paragraph shall be available solely to support, maintain, improve, and provide for the full operation for modernized creation, retention, and retrieval of information in each county's system of recorded documents.***

§ 27361.5. (a) As used in Section 27361, a page shall be one printed side of a single piece of paper being 8 1/2 inches by 11 inches.

(b) A sheet shall be one printed side of a single piece of paper which is not exactly 8 1/2 inches by 11 inches but not greater than 8 1/2 inches by 14 inches.

§ 66436. (a) A statement, signed and acknowledged by all parties having any record title interest in the subdivided real property, consenting to the preparation and recordation of the final map is required, ***

(c) A notary acknowledgment shall be deemed complete for recording without the official seal of the notary, so long as the name of the notary, the county of the notary's principal place of business, and the notary's commission expiration date are typed or printed below or immediately adjacent to the notary's signature in the acknowledgment.

Business and Professions Code

§ 6125. No person shall practice law in California unless the person is an active member of the State Bar.

§ 6126. (a) Any person advertising or holding himself or herself out as practicing or entitled to practice law or otherwise practicing law who is not an active member of the State Bar, is guilty of a misdemeanor. **•••**

§ 6127. The following acts or omissions in respect to the practice of law are contempts of the authority of the courts:

(a) Assuming to be an officer or attorney of a court and acting as such, without authority.

(b) Advertising or holding oneself out as practicing or as entitled to practice law or otherwise practicing law in any court, without being an active member of the State Bar.

Proceedings to adjudge a person in contempt of court under this section are to be taken in accordance with the provisions of Title V of Part III of the Code of Civil Procedure.

§ 22442.2. (a) An immigration consultant shall conspicuously display in his or her office a notice that shall be at least 12 inches by 20 inches with boldface type or print with each character at least one inch in height and width in English and in the native language of the consultant's clientele, the following information:

(1) The full name, address, and evidence of compliance with any applicable bonding requirement including the bond number, if any.

(2) A statement that the consultant is not an attorney.

(b) Prior to providing any services, an immigration consultant shall provide the client with written disclosure which shall include the immigration consultant's name, address, telephone number, agent for service of process, and evidence of compliance with any applicable bonding requirement, including the bond number, if any.

§ 22442.3. An immigration consultant shall not, with the intent to mislead, literally translate, from English into another language, the words or titles, including, but not limited to, "notary public," "notary," "licensed," "attorney," "lawyer," or any other terms that imply that the person is an attorney, in any document, including an advertisement, stationery, letterhead, business card, or other comparable written material describing the immigration consultant.

(b) For purposes of this section, "literal translation" of a word or phrase from one language means the translation of a word or phrase without regard to the true meaning of the word or phrase in the language that is being translated.

(c) An immigration consultant may not make or authorize the making of any verbal or written references to his or her compliance with the bonding requirements of Section 22443.1 except as provided in this chapter.

Civil Code

§ 14. Words used in this code in the present tense include the future as well as the present; words used in the masculine gender include the feminine and neuter; the singular number includes the plural, and the plural the singular; the word person includes a corporation as well as a natural person; county includes city and county; writing includes printing and typewriting; oath includes affirmation or declaration; and every mode of oral statement, under oath or affirmation, is embraced by the term "testify," and every written one in the term "depose"; signature or subscription includes mark, when the person cannot write, his name being written near it, by a person who writes his own name as a witness; provided, that when a signature is by mark it must in order that the same may be acknowledged or may serve as the signature to any sworn statement be witnessed by two persons who must subscribe their own names as witnesses thereto. ***

§ 1181. The proof or acknowledgment of an instrument may be made before a notary public at any place within this state, or within the county or city and county in this state in which the officer specified below was elected or appointed, before either:

(a) A clerk of a superior, municipal, or justice court.

(b) A county clerk.

(c) A court commissioner.

(d) A judge or retired judge of a municipal or justice court.

(e) A district attorney.

(f) A clerk of a board of supervisors.

(g) A city clerk.

(h) A county counsel.

(i) A city attorney.

§ 1182. The proof or acknowledgment of an instrument may be made without this state, but within the United States, and within the jurisdiction of the officer, before any of the following:

(1) A justice, judge, or clerk of any court of record of the United States.

(2) A justice, judge, or clerk of any court of record of any state.

(3) A commissioner appointed by the Governor or Secretary of State for that purpose.

(4) A notary public.

(5) Any other officer of the state where the acknowledgment is made authorized by its laws to take such proof or acknowledgment.

§ 1183. The proof or acknowledgment of an instrument may be made without the United States, before any of the following:

(a) A minister, commissioner, or charge d'affaires of the United States, resident and accredited in the country where the proof or acknowledgment is made.

(b) A consul, vice consul, or consular agent of the United States, resident in the country where the proof or acknowledgment is made.

(c) A judge of a court of record of the country where the proof or acknowledgment is made.

(d) Commissioners appointed by the Governor or Secretary of State for that purpose.

(e) A notary public.

If the proof or acknowledgment is made before a notary public, the signature of the notary public shall be proved or acknowledged (1) before a judge of a court of record of the country where the proof or acknowledgment is made, or (2) by any American diplomatic officer, consul general, consul, vice consul, or consular agent, or (3) by an apostille (certification) affixed to the instrument pursuant to the terms of The Hague Convention Abolishing the Requirement of Legalization for Foreign Public Documents.

§ 1183.5. Any officer on active duty or performing inactive-duty training in the armed forces having the general powers of a notary public pursuant to Section 936 or 1044a of Title 10 of the United States Code (Public Law 90-632 and 101-510) and any successor statutes may perform all notarial acts for any person serving in the armed forces of the United States, wherever he or she may be, or for any spouse of a person serving in the armed forces, wherever he or she may be, or for any person eligible for legal assistance under laws and regulations of the United States, wherever he or she may be, for any person serving with, employed by, or accompanying such armed forces outside the United States and outside the Canal Zone, Puerto Rico, Guam and the Virgin Islands, and any person subject to the Uniform Code of Military Justice outside of the United States.

Any instrument acknowledged by any such officer or any oath or affirmation made before such officer shall not be rendered invalid by the failure to state therein the place of execution or acknowledgment. No seal or authentication of the officer's certificate of acknowledgment or of any jurat signed by him or her shall be required but the officer taking the acknowledgment shall endorse thereon or attach thereto a certificate substantially in a form authorized by the laws of this state or in the following form:

On this the ___ day of ____, 19_, before me ____, the undersigned officer, personally appeared ____ known to me (or satisfactorily proven) to be (a) serving in the armed forces of the United States, (b) a spouse of a person serving in the armed forces of the United States, or (c) a person serving with, employed by, or accompanying the armed forces of the United States outside the United States and outside the Canal Zone, Puerto Rico, Guam, and the Virgin Islands, and to be the person whose name is subscribed to the within instrument and acknowledged that he or she executed the same. And the undersigned does further certify that he or she is at the date of this certificate a commissioned officer of the armed forces of the United States having the general powers of a notary public under the provisions of Section 936 or 1044a of Title 10 of the United States Code (Public Law 90-632 and 101-510).

_____ Signature of officer,
_____ rank, branch of service
and capacity in which signed.

To any affidavit subscribed and sworn to before such officer there shall be attached a jurat substantially in the following form:

Subscribed and sworn to before me on this ___ day of _____, 19_.
_____ Signature of officer,
_____ rank, branch of service
and capacity in which signed.

The recitals contained in any such certificate or jurat shall be prima facie evidence of the truth thereof, and any certificate of acknowledgment, oath or affirmation purporting to have been made by any commissioned officer of the Army, Air Force, Navy, Marine Corps or Coast Guard shall, notwithstanding the omission of any specific recitals therein, constitute presumptive evidence of the existence of the facts necessary to authorize such acknowledgment, oath or affirmation to be taken by the certifying officer pursuant to this section.

§ 1185. (a) The acknowledgment of an instrument shall not be taken unless the officer taking it personally knows, or has satisfactory evidence that the person making the acknowledgment is, the individual who is described in and who executed the instrument.

(b) For purposes of this article, "personally knows" means having an acquaintance, derived from association with the individual in relation to other people and based upon a chain of circumstances surrounding the individual, which establishes the individual's identity with at least reasonable certainty.

(c) For the purposes of this section "satisfactory evidence" means the absence of any information, evidence, or other circumstances which would lead a reasonable person to believe that the person making the acknowledgment is not the individual he or she claims to be and any one of the following:

(1) The oath or affirmation of a credible witness personally known to the officer that the person making the acknowledgment is personally known to the witness and that each of the following are true:

(A) The person making the acknowledgment is the person named in the document.

(B) The person making the acknowledgment is personally known to the witness.

(C) That it is the reasonable belief of the witness that the circumstances of the person making the acknowledgment are such that it would be very difficult or impossible for that person to obtain another form of identification.

(D) The person making the acknowledgment does not possess any of the identification documents named in paragraphs (3) and (4).

(E) The witness does not have a financial interest in the document being acknowledged and is not named in the document.

(2) The oath or affirmation under penalty of perjury of two credible witnesses, whose identities are proven to the officer upon the presentation of satisfactory evidence, that each statement in paragraph (1) of this subdivision is true.

(3) Reasonable reliance on the presentation to the officer of any one of the following, if the document is current or has been issued within five years:

(A) An identification card or driver's license issued by the California Department of Motor Vehicles.

(B) A passport issued by the Department of State of the United States.

(4) Reasonable reliance on the presentation of any one of the following, provided that a document specified in subparagraphs (A) to (E), inclusive, shall either be current or have been issued within five years and shall contain a photograph and description of the person named on it, shall be signed by the person, shall bear a serial or other identifying number, and, in the event that the document is a passport, shall have been stamped by the United States Immigration and Naturalization Service:

(A) A passport issued by a foreign government.

(B) A driver's license issued by a state other than California or by a Canadian or Mexican public agency authorized to issue drivers' licenses.

(C) An identification card issued by a state other than California.

(D) An identification card issued by any branch of the armed forces of the United States.

(E) An inmate identification card issued on or after January 1, 1988, by the Department of Corrections, if the inmate is in custody.

(F) An inmate identification card issued prior to January 1, 1988, by the Department of Corrections, if the inmate is in custody.

(d) An officer who has taken an acknowledgment pursuant to this section shall be presumed to have operated in accordance with the provisions of law.

(e) Any party who files an action for damages based on the failure of the officer to establish the proper identity of the person making the acknowledgment shall have the burden of proof in establishing the negligence or misconduct of the officer.

(f) Any person convicted of perjury under this section shall forfeit any financial interest in the document.

§ 1188. An officer taking the acknowledgment of an instrument shall endorse thereon or attach thereto a certificate substantially in the form prescribed in Section 1189.

§ 1189. (a) Any certificate of acknowledgment taken within this state shall be in substantially the following form:

> State of California)
> County of _____)
> On _____ before me, (here insert name and title of the officer), personally appeared _____, personally known to me (or proved to me on the basis of satisfactory evidence) to be the person(s) whose name(s) is/are subscribed to the within instrument and acknowledged to me that he/she/they executed the same in his/her/their authorized capacity(ies), and that by his/her/their signature(s) on the instrument the person(s), or the entity upon behalf of which the person(s) acted, executed the instrument.
> WITNESS my hand and official seal.
> Signature _____ (Seal)

(b) Any certificate of acknowledgment taken in another place shall be sufficient in this state if it is taken in accordance with the laws of the place where the acknowledgment is made.

(c) On documents to be filed in another state or jurisdiction of the United States, a California notary public may complete any acknowledgment form as may be required in that other state or jurisdiction on a document, provided the form does not require the notary to determine or certify that the signer holds a particular representative capacity or to make other determinations and certifications not allowed by California law.

(d) An acknowledgment provided prior to January 1, 1993, and conforming to applicable provisions of former Sections 1189, 1190, 1190a, 1190.1, 1191, and 1192, as repealed by Chapter 335 of the Statutes of 1990, shall have the same force and effect as if those sections had not been repealed.

§ 1190. The certificate of acknowledgment of an instrument executed on behalf of an incorporated or unincorporated entity by a duly authorized person in the form specified in Section 1189 shall be prima facie evidence that the instrument is the duly authorized act of the entity named in the instrument and shall be conclusive evidence thereof in favor of any good faith purchaser, lessee, or encumbrancer. "Duly authorized person," with respect to a domestic or foreign corporation, includes the president, vice president, secretary, and assistant secretary of the corporation.

§ 1193. Officers taking and certifying acknowledgments or proof of instruments for record, must authenticate their certificates by affixing thereto their signatures, followed by the names of their offices; also, their seals of office, if by the laws of the State or country where the acknowledgment or proof is taken, or by authority of which they are acting, they are required to have official seals.

§ 1195. Proof of the execution of an instrument, when not acknowledged, may be made either:

1. By the party executing it, or either of them; or
2. By a subscribing witness; or

3. By other witnesses, in cases mentioned in Section 1198.

§ 1196. If by a subscribing witness, that witness shall be personally known to the officer taking the proof to be the person whose name is subscribed to the instrument as a witness, or shall be proved to be such by the oath of a credible witness who is personally known to the officer taking the proof, as defined in subdivision (b) of Section 1185.

§ 1197. The subscribing witness must prove that the person whose name is subscribed to the instrument as a party is the person described in it, and that such person executed it, and that the witness subscribed his name thereto as a witness.

Code of Civil Procedure

§ 1935. A subscribing witness is one who sees a writing executed or hears it acknowledged, and at the request of the party thereupon signs his name as a witness.

§ 2025. *

(k) Except as provided in paragraph (3) of subdivision (d) of Section 2020, the deposition shall be conducted under the supervision of an officer who is authorized to administer an oath. This officer shall not be financially interested in the action and shall not be a relative or employee of any attorney of any of the parties, or of any of the parties. Any objection to the qualifications of the deposition officer is waived unless made before the deposition begins or as soon thereafter as the ground for that objection becomes known or could be discovered by reasonable diligence.

(l) (1) The deposition officer shall put the deponent under oath. Unless the parties agree or the court orders otherwise, the testimony, as well as any stated objections, shall be taken stenographically. The party noticing the deposition may also record the testimony by audiotape or videotape if the notice of deposition stated an intention also to record the testimony by either of those methods, or if all the parties agree that the testimony may also be recorded by either of those methods. Any other party, at that party's expense, may make a simultaneous audiotape or videotape record of the deposition, provided that other party promptly, and in no event less than three calendar days before the date for which the deposition is scheduled, serves a written notice of this intention to audiotape or videotape the deposition testimony on the party or attorney who noticed the deposition, on all other parties or attorneys on whom the deposition notice was served under subdivision (c), and on any deponent whose attendance is being compelled by a deposition subpoena under Section 2020. If this notice is given three calendar days before the deposition date, it shall be made by personal service under Section 1011. Examination and cross-examination of the deponent shall proceed as permitted at trial under the provisions of the Evidence Code. ***

§ 2026. *

(c) A deposition taken under this section shall be conducted (1) under the supervision of a person who is authorized to administer oaths by the laws of the United States or those of the place where the examination is to be held, and who is not otherwise disqualified under subdivision (k) of Section 2025, or (2) before a person appointed by the court. This appointment is effective to authorize that person to administer oaths and to take testimony. When necessary or convenient, the court shall issue a commission on such terms and with such directions as are just and appropriate. ***

§ 2027. *

(c) A deposition taken under this section shall be conducted (1) under the supervision of a person who is authorized to administer oaths or their equivalent by the laws of the United States or of the foreign nation, and who is not otherwise disqualified under subdivision (k) of Section 2025, or (2) a person or officer appointed by commission or under letters rogatory; or (3) any person agreed to by all the parties. *******

§ 2093. (a) Every court, every judge, or clerk of any court, every justice, and every notary public, and every officer or person authorized to take testimony in any action or proceeding, or to decide upon evidence, has the power to administer oaths or affirmations.

(b) Every shorthand reporter certified pursuant to Article 3 (commencing with Section 8020) of Chapter 13 of Division 3 of the Business and Professions Code has the power to administer oaths or affirmations and may perform the duties of the deposition officer pursuant to Section 2025. The certified shorthand reporter shall be entitled to receive fees for services rendered during a deposition, including fees for deposition services, as specified in subdivision (c) of Section 8211 of the Government Code.

(c) A former judge or justice of a court of record in this state who retired or resigned from office, other than a judge or justice who was retired by the Supreme Court for disability, shall have the power to administer oaths or affirmations, if the former judge or justice requests and receives a certification from the Commission on Judicial Performance that there was no formal disciplinary proceeding pending at the time of retirement or resignation. Where no formal disciplinary proceeding was pending at the time of retirement or resignation, the Commission on Judicial Performance shall issue the certification.

No law, rule, or regulation regarding the confidentiality of proceedings of the Commission on Judicial Performance shall be construed to prohibit the Commission on Judicial Performance from issuing a certificate as provided for in this section.

§ 2094. An oath, or affirmation, in an action or proceeding, may be administered as follows, the person who swears, or affirms, expressing his assent when addressed in the following form: "You do solemnly swear (or affirm, as the case may be), that the evidence you shall give in this issue (or matter), pending between ____ and ____, shall be the truth, the whole truth, and nothing but the truth, so help you God."

Elections Code

§ 8080. No fee or charge shall be made or collected by any officer for verifying any nomination document or circulator's affidavit.

Family Code

§ 503. The county clerk shall issue a confidential marriage license upon the request of a notary public approved by the county clerk to authorize confidential marriages pursuant to Chapter 2 (commencing with Section 530) and upon payment by the notary public of the fees specified in Sections 26840.1 and 26840.8 of the Government Code. The parties shall reimburse a notary public who authorizes a confidential marriage for the amount of the fees.

§ 530. (a) No notary public shall authorize a confidential marriage pursuant to this part unless the notary public is approved by the county clerk to authorize confidential marriages pursuant to this chapter.

(b) A violation of subdivision (a) is a misdemeanor punishable by a fine not to exceed one thousand dollars ($1,000) or six months in jail.

§ 531. (a) An application for approval to authorize confidential marriages pursuant to this part shall be submitted to the county clerk in the county in which the notary public who is applying for the approval resides.

(b) The application shall include all of the following:

(1) The full name of the applicant.

(2) The date of birth of the applicant.

(3) The applicant's current residential address and telephone number.

(4) The address and telephone number of the place where the applicant will issue authorizations for the performance of a marriage.

(5) The full name of the applicant's employer if the applicant is employed by another person.

(6) Whether or not the applicant has engaged in any of the acts specified in Section 8214.1 of the Government Code.

(c) The application shall be accompanied by the fee provided for in Section 536.

§ 532. No approval shall be granted pursuant to this chapter unless the notary public shows evidence of successful completion of a course of instruction concerning the authorization of confidential marriages that shall be conducted by the county clerk. The course of instruction shall not exceed two hours in duration.

§ 533. An approval to authorize confidential marriages pursuant to this chapter is valid for one year. The approval may be renewed for additional one-year periods upon payment of the renewal fee provided for in Section 536.

§ 534. (a) The county clerk shall maintain a list of the notaries public who are approved to authorize confidential marriages. The list shall be available for inspection by the public.

(b) It is the responsibility of a notary public approved to authorize confidential marriages pursuant to this chapter to keep current the information required in paragraphs (1), (3), (4), and (5) of subdivision (b) of Section 531. This information shall be used by the county clerk to update the list required to be maintained by this section.

§ 535. (a) If, after an approval to authorize confidential marriages is granted pursuant to this chapter, it is discovered that the notary public has engaged in any of the actions specified in Section 8214.1 of the Government Code, the approval shall be revoked, and any fees paid by the notary public may be retained by the county clerk.

(b) If a notary public who is approved to authorize confidential marriages pursuant to this chapter is alleged to have violated a provision of this division, the county clerk shall conduct a hearing to determine if the approval of the notary public should be suspended or revoked. The notary public may present such evidence as is necessary in the notary public's defense. If the county clerk determines that the notary public has violated a provision of this division, the county clerk may place the notary public on probation or suspend or revoke the notary public's registration, and any fees paid by the notary public may be retained by the county clerk. The county clerk shall report the findings of the hearing to the Secretary of State for whatever action the Secretary of State deems appropriate.

§ 536. (a) The fee for an application for approval to authorize confidential marriages pursuant to this chapter is one hundred seventy-five dollars ($175).

(b) The fee for a renewal of an approval is one hundred seventy-five dollars ($175).

(c) Fees received pursuant to this chapter shall be deposited in a trust fund established by the county clerk. The money in the trust fund shall be used exclusively for the administration of the program described in this chapter.

Penal Code

§ 17. (a) A felony is a crime which is punishable with death or by imprisonment in the state prison. Every other crime or public offense is a misdemeanor except those offenses that are classified as infractions. *******

§ 115.5. (a) Every person who files any false or forged document or instrument with the county recorder which affects title to, places an encumbrance on, or places an interest secured by a mortgage or deed of trust on, real property consisting of a single-family residence containing not more than four dwelling units, with knowledge that the document is false or forged, is punishable, in addition to any other punishment, by a fine not exceeding seventy-five thousand dollars ($75,000).

(b) Every person who makes a false sworn statement to a notary public, with knowledge that the statement is false, to induce the notary public to perform an improper notarial act on an instrument or document affecting title to, or placing an encumbrance on, real property consisting of a single-family residence containing not more than four dwelling units is guilty of a felony.

§ 118. (a) Every person who, having taken an oath that he or she will testify, declare, depose, or certify truly before any competent tribunal, officer, or person, in any of the cases in which the oath may by law of the State of California be administered, willfully and contrary to the oath, states as true any material matter which he or she knows to be false, and every person who testifies, declares, deposes, or certifies under penalty of perjury in any of the cases in which the testimony, declarations, depositions, or certification is permitted by law of the State of California under penalty of perjury and willfully states as true any material matter which he or she knows to be false, is guilty of perjury.

This subdivision is applicable whether the statement, or the testimony, declaration, deposition, or certification is made or subscribed within or without the State of California.

(b) No person shall be convicted of perjury where proof of falsity rests solely upon contradiction by testimony of a single person other than the defendant. Proof of falsity may be established by direct or indirect evidence.

§ 126. Perjury is punishable by imprisonment in the state prison for two, three or four years.

§ 472. Every person who, with intent to defraud another, forges, or counterfeits the seal of this State, the seal of any public officer authorized by law, the seal of any Court of record, or the seal of any corporation, or any other public seal authorized or recognized by the laws of this State, or of any other State, Government, or country, or who falsely makes, forges, or counterfeits any impression purporting to be an impression of any such seal, or who has in his possession any such counterfeited seal or impression thereof, knowing it to be counterfeited, and willfully conceals the same, is guilty of forgery.

§ 473. Forgery is punishable by imprisonment in the state prison, or by imprisonment in the county jail for not more than one year.

§ 653.55. It is a misdemeanor for any person for compensation to knowingly make a false or misleading material statement or assertion of fact in the preparation of an immigration matter which statement or assertion is detrimentally relied upon by another. Such a misdemeanor is punishable by imprisonment in the county jail not exceeding six months, or by a fine not exceeding two thousand five hundred dollars ($2,500), or by both.

§ 830.3. The following persons are peace officers whose authority extends to any place in the state for the purpose of performing their primary duty or when making an arrest pursuant to Section 836 of the Penal Code as to any public offense with respect to which there is immediate danger to person or property, or of the escape of the perpetrator of that offense, or pursuant to Section 8597 or 8598 of the Government Code. ***

(o) Investigators of the office of the Secretary of State designated by the Secretary of State, provided that the primary duty of these peace officers shall be the enforcement of the law as prescribed in Chapter 3 (commencing with Section 8200) of Division 1 of Title 2 of, and Section 12172.5 of, the Government Code.***

Probate Code

§ 4121. A power of attorney is legally sufficient if all of the following requirements are satisfied:

(a) The power of attorney contains the date of its execution.

(b) The power of attorney is signed either (1) by the principal or (2) in the principal's name by some other person in the principal's presence and at the principal's direction.

(c) The power of attorney is either (1) acknowledged before a notary public or (2) signed by at least two witnesses who satisfy the requirements of Section 4122.

§ 4122. If the power of attorney is signed by witnesses, as provided in Section 4121, the following requirements shall be satisfied:

(a) The witnesses shall be adults.

(b) The attorney-in-fact may not act as a witness.

(c) Each witness signing the power of attorney shall witness either the signing of the instrument by the principal or the principal's acknowledgment of the signature or the power of attorney.

(d) In the case of a durable power of attorney for health care, the additional requirements of Section 4701.

§ 4307. (a) A copy of a power of attorney certified under this section has the same force and effect as the original power of attorney.

(b) A copy of a power of attorney may be certified by any of the following:

(1) An attorney authorized to practice law in this state.

(2) A notary public in this state.

(3) An official of a state or of a political subdivision who is authorized to make certifications.

(c) The certification shall state that the certifying person has examined the original power of attorney and the copy and that the copy is a true and correct copy of the original power of attorney.

(d) Nothing in this section is intended to create an implication that a third person may be liable for acting in good faith reliance on a copy of a power of attorney that has not been certified under this section.

§ 4701. If the durable power of attorney for health care is signed by witnesses, as provided in Section 4121, in addition to the requirements applicable to witnesses under Section 4122, the following requirements shall be satisfied: ***

(e) If the principal is a patient in a skilled nursing facility, as defined in subdivision (c) of Section 1250 of the Health and Safety Code, at the time the durable power of attorney for health care is executed, the power of attorney is not effective unless a patient advocate or ombudsman as may be designated by the Department of Aging for this purpose pursuant to any other applicable provision of law signs the instrument as a witness, either as one of two witnesses or in addition to notarization pursuant to subdivision (c) of Section 4121. The patient advocate or ombudsman shall declare that he or she is serving as a witness as required by this subdivision. It is the intent of this subdivision to recognize that some patients in skilled nursing facilities are insulated from a voluntary decisionmaking role, by virtue of the custodial nature of their care, so as to require special assurance that they are capable of willfully and voluntarily executing a durable power of attorney for health care.

Uniform Commercial Code

§ 3505.***

(b) A protest is a certificate of dishonor made by a United States consul or vice consul, or a notary public or other person authorized to administer oaths by the law of the place where dishonor occurs. It may be made upon information satisfactory to that person. The protest shall identify the instrument and certify either that presentment has been made or, if not made, the reason why it was not made, and that the instrument has been dishonored by nonacceptance or nonpayment. The protest may also certify that notice of dishonor has·been given to some or all parties.

Welfare and Institutions Code

§ 11350.6. (a) As used in this section: ***

(2) "Board" means any *** state commission, department, committee, examiner, or agency that issues a license, certificate, credential, permit, registration, or any other authorization to engage in a business, occupation, or profession. ***

(5) "License" includes membership in the State Bar, and a certificate, credential, permit, registration, or any other authorization issued by a board that allows a person to engage in a business, occupation, or profession, or to operate a commercial motor vehicle, including appointment and commission by the Secretary of State as a notary public. ***

(6) "Licensee" means any person holding a license, certificate, credential, permit, registration, or other authorization issued by a board, to engage in a business, occupation, or profession, or a commercial driver's license as defined in Section 15210 of the Vehicle Code, including an appointment and commission by the Secretary of State as a notary public. ***

(e)(1) Promptly after receiving the certified consolidated list from the State Department of Social Services, and prior to the issuance or renewal of a license, each board shall determine whether the applicant is on the most recent certified consolidated list provided by the State Department of Social Services. The board shall have the authority to withhold issuance or renewal of the license of any applicant on the list.

(2) If an applicant is on the list, the board shall immediately serve notice as specified in subdivision (f) on the applicant of the board's intent to withhold issuance or renewal of the license. The notice shall be made personally or by mail to the applicant's last known mailing address on file with the board. Service by mail shall be complete in accordance with Section 1013 of the Code of Civil Procedure. ***

(C) In the event that a license or application for a license or the renewal of a license is denied pursuant to this section, any funds paid by the applicant or licensee shall not be refunded by the board. *** ∎

Office of the California Secretary of State

Sacramento

Mailing Address:
Secretary of State
Notary Public Section
P.O. Box 942877
Sacramento, CA 94277-0001
Telephone: 1-916-653-3595
Web site: www.ss.ca.gov

Street Address:
Secretary of State
Notary Public Section
1500 11th St., 2nd Floor
Sacramento, CA 95814

Fresno
Fresno Office
Secretary of State
2497 W. Shaw, Suite 101
Fresno, CA 93711
1-209-243-2100

Los Angeles
Los Angeles Office
Secretary of State
300 South Spring Street
12th Floor, South Tower
Los Angeles, CA 90013
1-213-897-5764

San Diego
San Diego Office
Secretary of State
1350 Front Street, Suite 2060
San Diego,CA 92101
1-619-525-4113

San Francisco
San Francisco Office
Secretary of State
235 Montgomery Street
Suite 725
San Francisco, CA 94104
1-415-439-6959

County Clerks' Offices

Upon receiving a new commission, the Notary must file an oath of office and bond with the County Clerk's office in the county of the Notary's principal place of business. The oath and bond must be filed within 30 days of the commission starting date.

At these same offices, certificates authenticating a local Notary's signature and seal may be obtained by anyone presenting a document notarized by the particular local Notary.

For certified copies of marriage certificates, contact the office of the County Clerk where the certificate was filed.

Alameda County
1221 Oak St., #249
Oakland 94612
1-510-272-6363

Alpine County
P.O. Box 158
Markleeville 96120
1-916-694-2281

Amador County
500 Argonaut Lane
Jackson 95642
1-209-223-6468

Butte County
25 County Center Dr.
Oroville 95965
1-530-538-7691

Calaveras County
Government Center
San Andreas 95249
1-209-754-6310

Colusa County
Courthouse
546 Jay St.
Colusa 95932
1-916-458-0500

Contra Costa County
823 Marina Vista
Martinez 94553
1-510-646-2955

Del Norte County
450 H St., #182
Crescent City 95531
1-707-464-7205

El Dorado County
360 Fair Lane
Placerville 95667
1-530-621-5496

3368 Lake Tahoe Blvd.
#108
S. Lake Tahoe 96150
1-916-573-3408

Fresno County
2221 Kern St.
Fresno 93722
1-209-488-3375

Glenn County
526 W. Sycamore St.
P.O. Box 391
Willows 95988
1-530-934-6407

Humboldt County
825 Fifth St., #108
Eureka 95501
1-707-445-7593

Imperial County
940 Main St., #206
El Centro 92243-2865
1-760-339-4272

Inyo County
P.O. Drawer F
Independence 93526
1-760-878-0220

Kern County
1115 Truxtun Ave.
Bakersfield 93301
1-805-861-2331

Kings County
Government Center
1400 W. Lacey Blvd.
Hanford 93230
1-209-582-3211, Ex. 2470

Lake County
255 N. Forbes St.
Lakeport 95453
1-707-263-2311

Lassen County
Courthouse
220 S. Lassen St.
Susanville 96130
1-530-251-8216

Los Angeles County
*Mailing address for all
L.A. County:*
Business Filing &
Registration
P.O. Box 53592
Los Angeles 90053-0592

*Walk-in addresses
(does not accept mail):*
335A East Avenue K6
Lancaster
1-805-723-4494

12400 E. Imperial Hwy.,
#1101
Norwalk
1-562-462-2177

14340 Sylvan St.
Van Nuys 91401
1-818-374-7191
1-818-374-7192

L.A. Municipal Court
Catalina Branch
215 Sumner Avenue
Avalon
1-310-510-0026

Madera County
209 W. Yosemite Ave.
Madera 93637
1-209-675-7720

Marin County
P.O. Box E
San Rafael 94913
1-415-499-6416

Mariposa County
Hall of Records
P.O. Box 247
Mariposa 95338
1-209-966-2621

Mendocino County
501 Low Gap Rd, #1020
Ukiah 95482
1-707-463-4370

Merced County
2222 M St.
Merced 95340
1-209-385-7511

Modoc County
204 Court St.
P.O. Box 131
Alturas 96101
1-916-233-6201

Mono County
P.O. Box 237
Bridgeport 93517
1-760-932-5242

Monterey County
240 Church St.
P.O. Box 29
Salinas 93902
1-408-755-5450

Napa County
P.O. Box 298
Napa 94559-0298
1-707-253-4105

Nevada County
10433 Willow Valley Rd.
Nevada City 95959-2347
1-916-265-1298

Orange County
630 N. Broadway
P.O. Box 238
Santa Ana 92702-0238
1-714-834-2222

Placer County
11544 C Ave.
P.O. Box 5278
Auburn 95604-5278
1-916-889-7100

Plumas County
P.O. Box 10207
Quincy 95971
1-916-283-6305

Riverside County
P.O. Box 751
Riverside 92502-0751
1-909-275-1949

Sacramento County
700 H St., #2720
Sacramento 95814
1-916-440-6705

San Benito County
Courthouse, Rm. 206
Hollister 95023
1-408-636-4029

San Bernardino County
172 W. 3rd St., 2nd Fl.
San Bernardino
92415-0302
1-909-387-6500

San Diego County
1600 Pacific Hwy., #260
P.O. Box 1750
San Diego 92101-2471
1-619-531-5507

334 Via Vera Cruz, #150
San Marcos 92069-2638
1-619-940-6868

5473 Kearny Villa Rd.
San Diego 92123-1160
1-619-505-6226

San Francisco County
25 Van Ness Ave., #110
San Francisco 94102
1-415-252-3282

San Joaquin County
24 S. Hunter, #304
P.O. Box 1968
Stockton 95201
1-209-468-2362

San Luis Obispo County
1144 Monterey St.
San Luis Obispo 93408
1-805-781-5228

San Mateo County
Fiscal Bldg.
2200 Broadway, 2nd Fl.
Redwood City 94063
1-650-363-4988

Santa Barbara County
County Admin. Bldg.
P.O. Box 159
Santa Barbara
93102-0159
1-805-568-2250

401 E. Cypress St., #108
Lompoc 93436
1-805-737-7899

511 E. Lakeside Pkwy.,
#115
Santa Maria 93455
1-805-346-8310

Santa Clara County
Superior Court Bldg.
191 N. First St.
San Jose 95113
1-408-299-2074

Santa Cruz County
701 Ocean St., #230
Santa Cruz 95060-4076
1-408-454-2060

Shasta County
P.O. Box 990880
1643 Market St.
Redding 96099
1-916-225-5378

Sierra County
Courthouse
P.O. Drawer D
Downieville 95936
1-916-289-3295

Siskiyou County
Courthouse
Box 338
Yreka 96097
1-916-842-8084

Solano County
Fiscal Bldg.
600 Texas St.
Fairfield 94533
1-707-421-7485

Sonoma County
2300 County Center Dr.,
#B177
Santa Rosa 95406
1-707-527-3800

Stanislaus County
1021 I St., #101
P.O. Box 1670 (95353)
Modesto 95354
1-209-525-5297

Sutter County
433 Second St.
Yuba City 95991
1-916-822-7120

Tehama County
P.O. Box 250
Red Bluff 96080
1-916-527-3350

Trinity County
P.O. Box 1258
Weaverville 96093-1258
1-916-623-1222

Tulare County
County Civic Center, #203
Visalia 93291-4593
1-209-733-6421

Tuolumne County
Admin. Center
2 S. Green St.
Sonora 95370
1-209-533-5551

Ventura County
Hall of Administration
Admin. Bldg. L, #1210
800 S. Victoria Avenue
Ventura 93009
1-805-654-2266

Yolo County
625 Court St., #B05
Woodland 95695
1-916-666-8264

Yuba County
935 14th St.
Marysville 95901
1-916-741-6341

Bureaus of Vital Statistics

California Notaries are not permitted to make certified copies of any document except powers of attorney and entries in their journals. Persons requesting notarization or certified copies of birth or death certificates should be referred to the respective state public office, below, that can provide certified copies of vital records. Persons requiring copies of foreign records should contact the appropriate consulate in the United States.

Alabama
Center for Health Statistics
State Dept. of Public Health
P.O. Box 5625
Montgomery, AL 36103-5625
1-205-242-5033

Alaska
Dept. of Health & Social Services
Bureau of Vital Statistics
P.O. Box H-02G
Juneau, AK 99811-0675
1-907-465-3391

Arizona
Vital Records Section
Arizona Dept. of Health Services
P.O. Box 3887
Phoenix, AZ 85030
1-602-255-3260

Arkansas
Div. of Vital Records, Dept. of Health
4815 West Markham St.
Little Rock, AR 72201
1-501-661-2336

California
Vital Statistics Section
Dept. of Health Services
P.O. Box 730241
Sacramento, CA 94244-0241
1-916-445-2684

Colorado
Vital Records Section, Dept. of Health
4300 Cherry Creek Drive South
Denver, CO 80222-1530
1-303-756-4464

Connecticut
Vital Records, Dept. of Health Services
150 Washington St.
Hartford, CT 06106
1-203-566-2334

Delaware
Office of Vital Statistics
Div. of Public Health
P.O. Box 637
Dover, DE 19903
1-302-739-4721

District of Columbia
Vital Records Branch
425 I St., N.W., Rm. 3009
Washington, DC 20001
1-202-727-9281

Florida
Dept. of Health & Rehabilitative Svs.
Office of Vital Statistics
1217 Pearl St.
P.O. Box 210
Jacksonville, FL 32231
1-850-359-6900

Georgia
Georgia Dept. of Human Resources
Vital Records Unit
47 Trinity Avenue, S.W., Rm. 217-H
Atlanta, GA 30334
1-404-656-4900

Hawaii
Office of Health Status Monitoring
State Dept. of Health
P.O. Box 3378
Honolulu, HI 96801
1-808-586-4533

Idaho
Vital Statistics Unit
Idaho Dept. of Health & Welfare
450 West State St.
Statehouse Mail
Boise, ID 83720-9990
1-208-334-5988

Illinois
Div. of Vital Records
Illinois Dept. of Public Health
605 West Jefferson St.
Springfield, IL 62702-5097
1-217-782-6553

Indiana
Vital Records Section
State Dept. of Health
1330 West Michigan St.
P.O. Box 1964
Indianapolis, IN 46206-1964
1-317-633-0274

Iowa
Iowa Dept. of Public Health
Vital Records Section, Lucas Ofc. Bldg.
321 East 12th St.
Des Moines, IA 50319-0075
1-515-281-4944

Kansas
Office of Vital Statistics
Kansas State Dept. of Health &
Environment
900 Jackson St.
Topeka, KS 66612-1290
1-913-296-1400

Kentucky
Office of Vital Statistics
Dept. for Health Services
275 East Main St.
Frankfort, KY 40621
1-502-564-4212

Louisiana
Vital Records Registry
Office of Public Health
325 Loyola Avenue
New Orleans, LA 70112
1-504-568-5152

Maine
Office of Vital Statistics
Maine Dept. of Human Services
State House Station 11
Augusta, ME 04333-0011
1-207-289-3184

Maryland
Div. of Vital Records
Dept. of Health & Mental Hygiene
Metro Executive Bldg.
4201 Patterson Ave.
P.O. Box 68760
Baltimore, MD 21215-0020
1-301-225-5988

Massachusetts
Registry of Vital Records & Statistics
150 Tremont St., Rm. B-3
Boston, MA 02111
1-617-727-7388

Michigan
Office of the State Registrar & Center
for Health Statistics
Michigan Dept. of Public Health
3423 North Logan St.
Lansing, MI 48909
1-517-335-8655

Minnesota
Minnesota Dept. of Health
Section of Vital Statistics
717 Delaware St., S.E.
P.O. Box 9441
Minneapolis, MN 55440
1-612-623-5121

Mississippi
Vital Records, State Dept. of Health
2423 North State St.
Jackson, MS 39216
1-601-960-7450

Missouri
Missouri Dept. of Health
Bureau of Vital Records
1730 East Elm
P.O. Box 570
Jefferson City, MO 65102-0570
1-314-751-6400

Montana
Bureau of Records & Statistics
State Dept. of Health & Environmental
Services
Helena, MT 59620
1-406-444-2614

Nebraska
Bureau of Vital Statistics
State Dept. of Health
301 Centennial Mall South
P.O. Box 95007
Lincoln, NE 68509-5007
1-402-471-2871

Nevada
Div. of Health – Vital Statistics
Capitol Complex
505 East King St., #102
Carson City, NV 89710
1-702-687-4480

New Hampshire
Bureau of Vital Records
Health and Welfare Bldg.
6 Hazen Drive
Concord, NH 03301
1-603-271-4654

New Jersey
State Dept. of Health
Bureau of Vital Statistics
South Warren and Market, CN 370
Trenton, NJ 08625
1-609-292-4087

New Mexico
Vital Statistics
New Mexico Health Services Div.
P.O. Box 26110
Santa Fe, NM 87502
1-505-827-2338

New York State
Vital Records Section
State Dept. of Health
Empire State Plaza, Tower Bldg.
Albany, NY 12237-0023
1-518-474-3075

New York City
Div. of Vital Records
New York City Dept. of Health
P.O. Box 3776
New York, NY 10007
1-212-693-4637

North Carolina
Dept. of Environment, Health &
Natural Resources
Div. of Epidemiology
Vital Records Section
225 North McDowell St., P.O. Box 29537
Raleigh, NC 27626-0537
1-919-733-3526

North Dakota
Div. of Vital Records
State Capitol
600 East Boulevard Avenue
Bismarck, ND 58505
1-701-224-2360

Ohio
Bureau of Vital Statistics
Ohio Dept. of Health
P.O. Box 15098
Columbus, OH 43215-0098
1-614-466-2531

Oklahoma
Oklahoma Vital Records Section
State Dept. of Health
1000 N.E. 10th St., P.O. Box 53551
Oklahoma City, OK 73152
1-405-271-4040

Oregon
Oregon Health Div.
Vital Statistics Section
P.O. Box 14050
Portland, OR 97214-0050
1-503-731-4095

Pennsylvania
Div. of Vital Records
State Dept. of Health, Central Bldg.
101 S. Mercer St., P.O. Box 1528
New Castle, PA 16103
1-412-656-3100

Rhode Island
Div. of Vital Records
Rhode Island Dept. of Health
Rm. 101, Cannon Bldg.
3 Capitol Hill
Providence, RI 02908-5097
1-401-277-2811

South Carolina
Office of Vital Records & Public
Health Statistics
South Carolina Dept. of Health &
Environmental Control
2600 Bull St.
Columbia, SC 29201
1-803-734-4830

South Dakota
State Dept. of Health
Center for Health Policy & Statistics
Vital Records
523 East Capitol
Pierre, SD 57501
1-605-773-3355

Tennessee
Tennessee Vital Records
Dept. of Health, Cordell Hull Bldg.
Nashville, TN 37247-0350
1-615-741-1763

Texas
Bureau of Vital Statistics
Texas Dept. of Health
1100 West 49th St.
Austin, TX 78756-3191
1-512-458-7111

Utah
Bureau of Vital Records
Utah Dept. of Health
288 North 1460 West
P.O. Box 16700
Salt Lake City, UT 84116-0700
1-801-538-6105

Vermont
Vermont Dept. of Health
Vital Records Section
60 Main St., Box 70
Burlington, VT 05402
1-802-828-3286

Virginia
Div. of Vital Records
State Health Dept.
P.O. Box 1000
Richmond, VA 23208-1000
1-804-786-6228

Washington
Dept. of Health
Center for Health Statistics
P.O. Box 9709
Olympia, WA 98507-9709
1-206-753-5936

West Virginia
Vital Registration Office
Div. of Health
State Capitol Complex, Bldg. 3
Charleston, WV 25305
1-304-558-2931

Wisconsin
Vital Records
1 West Wilson St.
P.O. Box 309
Madison, WI 53701
1-608-266-1371

Wyoming
Vital Records Services
Hathaway Bldg.
Cheyenne, WY 82002
1-307-777-7591

American Samoa
Registrar of Vital Statistics
Vital Statistics Section
Government of American Samoa
Pago Pago, AS 96799
1-684-633-1222, ext. 214

Guam
Office of Vital Statistics
Dept. of Public Health & Social
Services
Government of Guam
P.O. Box 2816
Agana, GU, M.I. 96910
1-671-734-4589

Northern Mariana Islands
Superior Court
Vital Records Section
P.O. Box 307
Saipan, MP 96950
1-670-234-6401, ext. 15

Panama Canal Zone
Panama Canal Commission
Vital Statistics Clerk
APOAA 34011

Puerto Rico
Dept. of Health
Demographic Registry
P.O. Box 11854
Fernández Juncos Station
San Juan, PR 00910
1-809-728-7980

Virgin Islands (St. Croix)
Registrar of Vital Statistics
Charles Harwood Memorial Hospital
Christiansted, St. Croix, VI 00820
1-809-774-9000, ext. 4621

**Virgin Islands (St. Thomas,
St. John)**
Registrar of Vital Statistics
Knud Hansen Complex
Hospital Ground
Charlotte Amalie
St. Thomas, VI 00802
1-809-774-9000, ext. 4621

Hague Convention Nations

The nations listed on the following pages are parties to a treaty called the Hague Convention Abolishing the Requirement of Legalization (Authentication) for Foreign Public Documents.

Treaty Simplifies Authentication. A Notary's signature on documents that are sent to these nations may be authenticated (verified as valid for the benefit of the recipient in the foreign nation) by California's Secretary of State through attachment of a single certificate of capacity called an *apostille*. The *apostille* (French for "notation") is the only authentication certificate necessary. Nations not subscribing to the Hague Convention may require as many as five or six separate authenticating certificates from different governmental agencies, domestic and foreign.

How to Request an *Apostille*. To obtain an *apostille*, anyone may mail the notarized document and a $20 check payable to the "Secretary of State" to:

> Office of Secretary of State
> Notary Public Section
> P.O. Box 942877
> Sacramento, CA 94277-0001

An *apostille* must be specifically requested, indicating the nation to which the document will be sent. In person, an *apostille* may be obtained at 1500 11th Street (second floor) in Sacramento, but the cost for an in-person request is $26.

It is *not* the Notary's responsibility to obtain an *apostille*, but rather, it is the responsibility of the party needing authentication.

Hague Convention Nations. The following nations participate in the Hague Convention:

Andorra	El Salvador
Angola[1]	Fiji
Antigua and Barbuda	Finland
Argentina[2]	France[5]
Armenia[3]	Germany
Australia	Greece
Austria	Grenada[1]
Bahamas	Guyana
Barbados	Hong Kong[6]
Belarus[3]	Hungary
Belgium	Israel
Belize	Italy
Bosnia-Herzegovina[4]	Japan
Botswana	Kiribati[1]
Brunei	Latvia
Comoros Islands[1]	Lesotho
Croatia[4]	Liberia[7]
Cyprus	Liechtenstein
Djibouti[1]	Luxembourg
Dominica[1]	Macedonia[4]

1. Recently independent country; has not confirmed that the Convention still applies. In accordance with Article 34(l) of the Vienna Convention on Succession of States in Respect of Treaties, the United States' view is that when a country is a party to a multilateral treaty or convention, and that country dissolves, the successor states inherit the treaty obligations of the former government.

2. Excludes recognition of extension of the Convention by the United Kingdom to the Malvinas, South Georgia, South Sandwich Islands and the Argentine Antarctic Sector.

3. Now known as the Newly Independent States. Former Union of Soviet Socialist Republics (U.S.S.R.) had signed on to the Convention, but dissolved prior to its taking effect. Only Armenia, the Belarus Republic and the Russian Federation of the former U.S.S.R. have confirmed that the Convention applies in their jurisdictions.

4. Former Yugoslavia, with its capital in the present Serbia-Montenegro, was a party to the Convention. However, only the breakaway nations of Bosnia-Herzegovina, Croatia, Macedonia and Slovenia have confirmed that the Convention still applies.

5. Including French Overseas Departments of French Guiana, French Polynesia, Guadeloupe, Martinique, New Caledonia, Reunion, St. Pierre and Miquelon, and Wallis and Futuna.

6. Retained status as Hague nation after control of Hong Kong was returned to China on July 1, 1997.

7. Convention does *not* apply between Liberia and the United States.

Malawi
Malta
Marshall Islands
Mauritius
Mexico
Mozambique[1]
Netherlands[8]
Norway
Panama
Portugal[9]
Russia[3]
Saint Kitts and Nevis
Saint Lucia
Saint Vincent and
   the Grenadines

San Marino, Republic of
Seychelles
Slovenia[4]
Solomon Islands[1]
South Africa
Spain
Suriname
Swaziland
Switzerland
Turkey
Tuvalu[1]
United Kingdom[10]
United States
   of America
Vanuatu[1]

Inquiries. Persons having questions about the Hague Convention Abolishing the Requirement of Legalization for Foreign Public Documents may address their inquiries to:

Office of American Citizen Services
Department of State
Washington, D.C. 20520
1-202-647-5225

---

1. Recently independent country; has not confirmed that the Convention still applies. In accordance with Article 34(1) of the Vienna Convention on Succession of States in Respect of Treaties, the United States' view is that when a country is a party to a multilateral treaty or convention, and that country dissolves, the successor states inherit the treaty obligations of the former government.

3. Now known as the Newly Independent States. Former Union of Soviet Socialist Republics (U.S.S.R.) had signed on to the Convention, but dissolved prior to its taking effect. Only Armenia, the Belarus Republic and the Russian Federation of the former U.S.S.R. have confirmed that the Convention applies in their jurisdictions.

4. Former Yugoslavia, with its capital in the present Serbia-Montenegro, was a party to the Convention. However, only the breakaway nations of Bosnia-Herzegovina, Croatia, Macedonia and Slovenia have confirmed that the Convention still applies.

8. Extended to Aruba, Curacao and Netherlands Antilles.

9. Extended to Macao and all overseas territories.

10. United Kingdom of Great Britain and Northern Ireland is extended to Anguilla, Bermuda, British Antarctica Territory, British Virgin Islands, Cayman Islands, Falkland Islands, Gibraltar, Guernsey, Isle of Man, Jersey, Montserrat, Saint Georgia and the South Sandwich Islands, Saint Helena, Tonga, Turks and Caicos Islands, and Zimbabwe.

About the Publisher

Since 1957, The National Notary Association — a nonprofit educational organization — has served the nation's nearly four and a half million Notaries Public with a wide variety of instructional programs and services.

As the country's clearinghouse for information on notarial laws, customs and practices, the NNA educates Notaries through publications, seminars, annual conferences and a *Notary Information Service* that offers immediate answers to specific questions about notarization.

The Association is perhaps most widely known as the preeminent publisher of information for and about Notaries. In addition, the National Notary Association provides Notaries with the highest quality professional supplies, including official seals and stamps, embossers, record-keeping journals, affidavit stamps, thumbprinting devices and notarial certificates.

Though dedicated primarily to educating and assisting Notaries, the National Notary Association devotes part of its resources to helping lawmakers draft effective notarial statutes and to informing the public about the Notary's vital role in modern society. ∎

Index

Page numbers listed in **bold** indicate where the most complete information on a subject can be found. *Italics* indicate the pages where the statutes pertaining to a subject are located.

C

Page numbers listed in **bold** indicate where the most complete information on a subject can be found. *Italics* indicate the pages where the statutes pertaining to a subject are located.

Page numbers listed in **bold** indicate where the most complete information on a subject can be found. *Italics* indicate the pages where the statutes pertaining to a subject are located.

O

P

N

Page numbers listed in **bold** indicate where the most complete information on a subject can be found. *Italics* indicate the pages where the statutes pertaining to a subject are located.